WINTER LIGHT

BEFORE YOU START TO READ THIS BOOK, take this moment to think about making a donation to punctum books, an independent non-profit press,

@ https://punctumbooks.com/support/

If you're reading the e-book, you can click on the image below to go directly to our donations site. Any amount, no matter the size, is appreciated and will help us to keep our ship of fools afloat. Contributions from dedicated readers will also help us to keep our commons open and to cultivate new work that can't find a welcoming port elsewhere. Our adventure is not possible without your support.

Vive la Open Access.

Fig. 1. Detail from Hieronymus Bosch, *Ship of Fools* (1490–1500)

Published in 2025 by punctum books, Earth, Milky Way.
https://punctumbooks.com

ISBN-13: 978-1-68571-224-2 (print)
ISBN-13: 978-1-68571-225-9 (ePDF)

DOI: 10.53288/0533.1.00

LCCN: 2025933116
Library of Congress Cataloging Data is available from the Library of Congress

Editing: Vincent W.J. van Gerven Oei and SAJ
Book design: Hatim Eujayl
Cover design: Vincent W.J. van Gerven Oei

punctumbooks

spontaneous acts of scholarly combustion

HIC SVNT MONSTRA

WINTER LIGHT

ON LATE LIFE'S
RADIANCE

DOUGLAS J. PENICK

p.

Contents

Acknowledgments

Everlasting thanks to Vincent W.J. van Gerven Oei and Eileen A. Fradenburg Joy and all the staff of punctum books who have been extraordinary in their great vision and dedication, not just to this book, but to so many remarkable and forward-looking texts.

I am utterly grateful to Deborah Marshall, Kidder Smith, Russell Bennetts, John Von Daler, James Shaheen, Gaetano Maeda, Van Penick, Noni Pratt, Steve Grad, Jacqueline Wurn, Bruce Blankenship, Starling Lawrence, Meg Federico, Stephen Brooks, Dan Cooper, Hazel Bercholz, Randy Sunday, Jim Mitchell, Louisa Ermelino, Brian Otte, Livy Snyder, and Milton Slater, among others, for their patient reading and generous advice.

Winter Light *is dedicated to Emilio Ambasz,*
il miglor fabro.

Without his continuous inspiration, conviction,
friendship, and generosity, and the support of the
LEAF Foundation, this book would not exist.

Preface

All of us have to learn the points of the compass again as often as we awake, whether from sleep or any abstraction. Not 'til we are lost […] not 'til we have lost the world, do we begin to find ourselves and realize where we are and the infinite extent of our relations.

— Henry David Thoreau, *Walden*1

[I]in appreciating the passage of time, the first step is the hardest.

— Marcel Proust, *Time Regained*2

Our old age is an experience of continuous and endless unfamiliarity.

— DJP

All at once and much to my surprise, I am old. I did not expect it, and it is not what I expected. The world in which I worked, struggled, dreamed, and loved now regards me quite differently than it did even ten years ago. Abruptly, I'm one in a large minority that is often ignored, frequently disdained, and regularly segregated. From the point of view of children, adolescents, and adults in general, I am no longer completely part of the world on the go. I am no longer a part of social groups in which I had a place. People dear to me decline precipitously and die. Familiar coffee shops, stores, parks, landmarks are gone. We now know we are subjects completely of time and change. Customs, fashions, beliefs, truths, even the future, all these have changed. It becomes clear in old age that we will not be establishing a stable way of existing in space or time. Navigating this altered world requires circumspection. By aging, it seems, we become exiles.

And this is not simply an outer experience. I now find myself estranged from the person I was accustomed to being. My body and senses weaken, become unreliable in unforeseen ways, fall subject to illness, and require more attention simply to continue a reasonable level of function. My world is marked by loss and uncertainty. My thinking, feeling, responding, imagining seem somehow unfamiliar. This is not how I thought of myself or my future. Things are no longer in my control. My life has become strangely unrecognizable. My world, my self are less stable, less secure. I have, even to myself, become somewhat "other."

Everything is more intensely transitory. But as the world becomes more distant and out of control, I begin to see patterns I had never imagined or only dimly sensed. Situations, objects, places, people become, moment by moment, very deeply to be cherished, valued; loved, not in spite of being impermanent, but because we are only together for this moment. It is like watching clouds move across the sky. Colors become more vivid, momentary smells more intense, sudden sounds abrupt. Temperatures and textures, memories, ideas, gestures appear, vanish, and only briefly detach themselves from the flow of sensoria. Other worlds, it seems, are waiting to show themselves.

* * *

My long-suffering piano teacher, Mr. Klaus Goetze, would sometimes play for his students, and one afternoon he performed Beethoven's Sonata in A-flat, No. 31, Op. 110. I was 17 and had already heard many of Beethoven's more popular sonatas in concert and on recordings, but nothing prepared me for what I heard him play. It changed my life in a subtle way, and now, some sixty years later, it has returned to inspire the explorations which have become this book.

Beethoven wrote this music when he was 50 years old; he was completely deaf, often very sick, and would die five years later. The order by which the sonata progressed was familiar, but its inner impulse was strangely austere, full of unfamiliar longing, searching, finding unsuspected ways forward, touching on new and unique kinds of resolution. Emotional changes and shifts of keys moved in ways both surprising and deeply moving. In the third and final movement, the grammar contained elements one could never have anticipated (a single note repeated eighteen times, a chord repeated ten times); the sorrow and resolution seemed to emanate from a vast and unfamiliar expanse on the edge of silence. It was not just the notes, but the space from which they emerged, where they reverberated and in which finally they ended that was transformative. Nothing has ever erased the shock of being drawn into a terrain of such intensity, depth, possibility, and loss. Looking at Beethoven's life when he wrote this may provide some context for the piece but does not explain how he achieved this.

LUDWIG VAN BEETHOVEN (1770–1827)

Beethoven was an almost unbearable person: willful, extravagantly self-absorbed, angry, inconsiderate, demanding, harsh, often close to feral. As Lewis Lockwood has put it: "Two elements of Beethoven's domestic life run through his last ten years like persistent motives from one of his major works: isolation and obsessiveness."[3] Even in the "fallow period" between 1812 and 1817, "personal complications contributed to slowing Beethoven's creative work, but his drastically changing artistic outlook contributed even more."[4] He looked to the past, to the counterpoint of Bach and Handel in order to "open up and deepen new perspectives on his own development."[5]

His hearing had deteriorated almost completely. Deafness constricts our sense of ambient space; putting one's fingers in one's ears makes this loss evident. Space behind and to the sides pulls in. This creates a compressed dimension of inner space and could only have intensified Beethoven's retreat into himself and the inwardness of his music. Lockwood writes:

> The further decline in Beethoven's health moved in tandem with his increasing psychological withdrawal and deepening anxiety. Here the emotional and intellectual demands that he made on himself expanded and deepened as he composed the last piano sonatas, the Ninth Symphony, the *Missa Solemnis* and the last quartets.[6]

Throughout the 1820s, Beethoven's health became even more unstable. He was afflicted by rheumatic fever, bowel complaints, jaundice, and inflammations in his eyes. Newspapers reported that his closest friends were concerned for his survival. There were times when he was barely recognizable.

> In early 1820, at the same time when he was composing Piano Sonata, Op. 110, he went for a long walk along a canal towpath outside of Vienna and made his way to a canal basin at Ungerthor. He had eaten nothing, was exhausted, confused, and disoriented; he began to look through the windows of houses near the path. He was so erratic and so shabbily dressed that the residents became alarmed and called the police. He proclaimed loudly to the officers that he was Beethoven, but he looked so much more like a beggar that he was not believed. They locked him up and held him until a nearby music teacher named Herzog, hearing about the unfortunate prisoner, came to look. He told the officers that this was indeed the famous composer. They gave him some clean clothing, food and ordered a cab to take him home.[7]

In that period, Gioachino Rossini, an equally famous composer who in old age also radically altered the style and aims of his work, came to call on Beethoven. In his brief account of the visit, he was clearly appalled by the malodorous squalor in which the great man lived, his lack of personal hygiene, and most of all his complete deafness. He did not stay long.[8] "When I descended those dilapidated stairs, I retained of my visit to this great man an impression so painful — thinking of this destitution and shabbiness — that I could not repress my tears," he remembered.[9]

On September 10, 1821, Beethoven wrote to his friend, Tobias Hanslinger:

> When I was in my carriage yesterday on the way to Vienna, sleep overpowered me, the more so as I had scarcely ever had a good night's sleep [...]. Now, as I was slumbering, I dreamed that I was travelling far away, to Arabia too, and at last I came even to Jerusalem. The Holy City reminded me of the Holy Scriptures; no wonder then that I thought of the man Tobias too [...]. Now during my dream journey the following canon occurred to me [...] to the following words: "O Tobias. O Tobias, Hoo! O! O Tobias." Yet I had hardly awoken when the tune and its canon was gone, and I could not recall a single note or word of it. However, when on the next day I returned here in the same carriage (that of a poor Austrian musician) and continued my dream journey, though now awake, lo and behold, in accord with the law of association of ideas, the same canon occurred to me; now, waking I held it fast, as once Menelaus held Proteus, and only granted it one last favor, that of allowing it to transform itself into three voices.[10]

Thus, trapped in silence, amid an instability intensified by personal losses, court cases, endless sickness, and occasional mental breakdown, Beethoven heard new music within the extremes of a life moving to its end. As his outer and inner world became increasingly unfamiliar, increasingly "other," he found himself looking beyond conventional boundaries and expectations. His music drew on further reserves of inwardness, entering ever deeper currents of grief, frustration, longing, and resolution. The music of this late period was, and has remained, profoundly mysterious, profoundly challenging, and an inexplicable won-

der. It seems Beethoven's music then was not invented or created, but discovered waiting in some deep, uncompromising
expanse of spirit. He never heard it in the world outside himself.

* * *

Now I am 79 years old. In the unfamiliar spaces revealed by
different kinds of loss, chance patterns emerge and resonate
momentarily. And, with whatever apprehension and sadness
this evokes, new perspectives, new kinds of beauty, new subtleties present themselves unsought. Old is, I have come to see, a
time of life that is uniquely and profoundly revealing. This, then,
has led to one aspect of this book: the world of what is often
called an artist's "late period," a time of artistic transformation
that unfolds as the end of life nears.

Winter Light explores inner discoveries that emerge in old
age and decline. The book focuses on artists, composers, architects, and writers, who have, in their last years, found a very different way of exploring their worlds and of conveying what they
found. For some, it was a completely new discovery, for others it was something they had glimpsed much earlier but only
found the means to realize as their life neared its end. Fredric
Jameson's comments on Van Gogh's famous painting of peasant
shoes (1886), illuminate in a general way how their art revealed
domains of unsuspected possibility within painful and degraded
circumstances. As he says, "the willed and violent transformation of a drab peasant object world into the most glorious mate-
rialization of pure colour in oil paint is to be seen as a Utopian
gesture: as an act of compensation which ends up producing a
whole new Utopian realm of the senses."[11] Here, within the inescapable brutality of our living and dying, art can reveal realms
of inherent possibility, luminosity, and vision. Thus, in their old
age, because they did not turn away from decay, desolation, and
loss, the artists discussed later were able to uncover expanses of
undreamt-of realities and new ways of sharing them.

To become old is to become "other" to oneself, "other" to
one's friends and family, to one's world. Losses have broken up

familiar boundaries, violated definitions, revealed unsuspected landscapes, opened ways of thinking and feeling previously unimagined. The onslaught of chaos has exposed new visual patterns, new associations in memory, new shapes and colors in the skies, unsuspected conceptual links, depths of yearning in the dark of night. This is the mystery which many artists in their old age found ways to explore.

This book is not, however, a guide to the intense and uncertain expanse before us; such a thing is not possible. Rather, this is a companion offered to all who are or will be in this last phase of life. It is hoped that as we grow old, experiencing ever more completely the unfamiliarity of ourselves and our world, we will discover new pathways and new dimensions to share with those of every age.

I

Body

Ripeness is all; her in her cooling planet
Revere; do not presume to think her wasted.
— William Empson, "To an Old Lady"[1]

The body is not a thing; it is a situation: it is our grasp on the world and the outline of our projects.
— Simone de Beauvoir, *The Second Sex*[2]

We […] can only access the truth of things because our body is embedded in them.
— Maurice Merleau-Ponty, "Exploring the World of Perception"[3]

Like the scent of ice at the end of fall, like the faint smell of green buds at winter's end, old age begins subtly, unexpectedly, and takes us almost unawares. One day we notice that our bodies, our passions are shifting in ways that are unfamiliar, disconcerting, shaky. We feel ourselves falter. Something is falling away. We are caught in an undertow. The world, it seems, is becoming the possession of others. We cannot hold on. Our time here, we suddenly suspect, is passing. We might wish to prolong earlier states of certainty and well-being, but it seems this is not possible. Our body somehow seems less dense, less tractable. Sudden, bone-weary fatigue. The world begins to move away. Everything around us seems now more translucent, more flickering.

No one has any idea of what it will mean to be old. As a discovery, it is disorienting. It is not something we were aiming for. It is not part of our sense of trajectory. But now, slowly, many aspects of ourselves that we had taken for granted are no longer stable. Our situation in our body, in our social life, in our ways of thinking is being altered. It is all in some ways familiar, of course, but in other ways not. And being old and getting older, this is not something we simply get used to. We are in an unpredictable state of continuous change. Things shift slowly then suddenly in major ways. We must change the ways we live to accommodate unplanned, unimaginable, and unwanted alterations. Less and less can we take anything for granted.

For these reasons, old age is also a time when our experience becomes more intense. A feeling of uncertainty underlies everything. Each of us becomes isolated in this. We become more alone and more wary. This is not just a matter of looking more carefully at the sidewalk, at oncoming traffic, at things relating to safety. It carries over into how we are aware of friends and family and their lives. It somehow makes the sky more brilliant, and hot weather more hot. Everything is sharper emotionally. And then, there is this: my wife is sleeping and suddenly I am overwhelmed and about to burst into tears. I don't know why. It is not a time, however, when we can hide much, particularly from ourselves.

As we are growing old, our body and world inexorably slip from our grasp and out of our control. Old age is marked by the most extreme losses, unknowns, the deepest and most intractable fears. Life is moving toward its end, even as the intensity of living continues. Being alive, living in this body and this world, walking home on a just too chilly early spring evening, this moment among so many others, has intense allure. We feel such a deep desire for it all, even if our desires do not take on quite the same form as earlier. Sexual desire, social and economic ambition do not vanish, they are just strangely altered, more tender, sad even. They are less at the forefront of a journey which is more and more taking us where it will. And we do not know where that is.

A very different space is opening before us. We are moving closer to dying. Subtly, obliquely, something alien is stirring in our body. We feel its slight advance even when, say, we are brushing our teeth. A sudden cramp in the hand. The brush falls into the sink. For a moment, there's a break in the morning continuum. An instant when we lose possession of what we expect is a sharp hint at something more absolute. It's a minute glimpse of larger loss. This does not displace our desires and longings; it places them in a different and more fragile context. So many momentary impulses, fears, yearnings have shaped us and are shaping us now. Now they flicker like constellations seen in the wide lightless depth of night. And we have a certain curiosity, a kind of unforced, unshaped appetite, binding us to these flickering patterns. Darkness and starlight intensify each other.

The revered Tibetan poet and yogi Milarepa made a song of it:

When old age descends upon you,
Your body, once straight, must bend down.
When you try to step forward firmly, you stagger.
Your hair turns white.
Your cheeks are pale.
Your eyes grow cloudy and dim.
Your hearing is muffled.
You shake and are dizzy.
Your blood dries up.
You cannot help stammering.

You are old and now death is approaching.
You are anguished and aware of how much you have depended on others.
Whatever wealth you accumulated, whatever friends you cultivated, whatever knowledge you picked up:

> You cannot keep them: they cannot help, and they abandon
> you.
> You try to ignore your suffering and pretend you can avoid
> your fate.
> You follow doctors and people who say they can save you,
> But your suffering increases.
> Now when you tell people what you experience,
> They do not want to know.
> You are alone.[4]

"The only real difference between people is their age," said the painter Edward Avedisian over a glass of gin. And in old age, the truth of this is clearer. All human beings have the same, almost identical experiences while defecating, urinating, swallowing, coughing, vomiting, cleaning their nose, itching, scratching, feeling hot or cold, experiencing the pain associated with stomach, lung, intestine, ear, eyes, etc. Desire, anger, fear, and indifference are likewise, in their basic momentum, identical from one person to the next. But these sensations and impulses present themselves, are experienced and expressed differently according to one's time of life.

Old age is, of course, a time of loss. There are, as everyone knows, the losses relating to our bodies, to our sense faculties, to our acuity. We do not feel or look the same. We become less appealing, even less lovable. For some of these, we can find compensations, for others there are no repairs. Seeing poorly, hearing poorly, not being able to walk far or run quickly, we find ourselves living with greater limitations in the world. The world itself becomes less accessible, and we are increasingly isolated within our body itself.

Indeed, deafness, tinnitus, macular degeneration, cataracts, and so forth become common with age. Hearing loss contracts ambient space. My sense of taste has changed rather than diminished. My sweet tooth remains, but my cooking of savory dishes is less sweet. I am now drawn to the range of tastes in sweet and hot peppers. Even though I stopped smoking only fifteen years ago, my sense of smell is acute, perhaps more to sour smells and slightly less to burnt ones. I am fortunate in that my eyesight is good. However, I notice that my sensitivity to yellow has decreased and to blue increased. The sensitivity of my night vision has declined, but darkness seems denser and somehow more textured. Hearing tests show a falling off in hearing upper frequencies, but I do not notice this in listening to, say, string quartets or singers. I am aware, however, of hearing bass registers with greater clarity. This inventory of changes can fill pages, but it is the impact of such difficulties that is of more significance.

Most studies into perception in the old focus on losses, deficits, and deviations from norms; there is less investigation of qualitative perceptual shifts. But these frequently occur. The great pianist Sviatoslav Richter said that in old age his pitch sensibility became a half to a whole tone sharper and that the same thing had affected his teacher, Heinrich Neuhaus, and Sergei Prokofiev as well. Mostly, of course, the changes in the registers of perception are not so extreme as to cause diminished functionality or can be accommodated in mechanical ways (hearing aids, glasses, changing the headlights on the car). But perceptual shifts change the world which we, the old, are seeing, hearing, smelling, and tasting. We are not living in the same perceptual world as once we did.

Old, it now seems that the senses are less tied to the solidity of the world outside. But not uniformly so. Sometimes our sense of smell and taste are noticeably less vibrant, our eyesight and hearing weaker and our sense of touch less sure in holding on to things. On other occasions, the scent of rhododendrons in spring, the sound of a clarinet next door, the taste of fresh figs, the sight of the slate blue sea just as the sun has set bring more intensity, as if life had just been born.

Sensations more often now bring with them resonances from the past. The early winter breeze brings back walking to school, winter by a river, skating on a frozen lake; the smell of lilacs on a warm breeze brings the thought of Walt Whitman, the yearning to fall in love, a sadness in spring; music faintly heard behind a closed door in a long musty corridor. No memory is a refuge; all are unresolved. On and on, in old age, our senses do not present us with one thing in one time, but many, resonating through time. The world is offering continuous and simultaneous perceptual pathways. And thus, we find ourselves in a deeper, less stable, less definable space.

My friend's 93-year-old father sat in the back yard in midsummer. "I never knew there were so many kinds of green," he smiled.

"Generally, as we age, the world shrinks," said the famed director André Gregory.

> Our creaky arthritic knees won't carry us far. Our friends begin to pass on. [...] A shrinking world is slowly burying us [...]. But through painting [...] I am now living a second childhood. [...] *Look.* Trees are so much more than green — black, yellow, red, umber. Depending on the light, all colors exist in everything. "Color," Paul Klee says, "links us with cosmic regions." [...] And shadows, shadows everywhere. Just look. And wonder. As I learn to look, the world appears richer, larger, more splendid.[5]

* * *

TITIAN (1488–1576)

Titian (Tiziano Vecelli) had a long, vigorous life of continuous triumph. He attracted the admiration and patronage of the most powerful figures in Europe, and even in his late seventies, when he changed his style radically, his work remained in great demand. There is in every painting, no matter his age and style, a vibrant curiosity about and sensuous responsiveness to his subjects.

Thomas Bernhard's novel, *Old Masters,* has an account of two old men who have tried and failed to find solace in the great European art works of the past. As one says of their famous makers: "They invariably painted a world of hypocrisy, hoping to get riches and fame; they all painted with this sole intention, driven by avarice and attention-seeking […] every single brush-stroke by these so-called Old Masters is a lie."[6] Titian, in almost all his letters and many of his reported meetings would seem to be a case in point. Unlike his contemporary, Michelangelo, who wrote many sonnets and whose letters are as often concerned with his inner life as with his working arrangements, Titian wrote letters that are almost all business; his inner thoughts are concealed within his social role and material needs.

In his correspondence with Phillip II of Spain, requesting more time and more money, Titian also frequently referred to his great old age in order to make his appeals more persuasive. In one letter, he said he was 95 and in another, not too much later, 103. Be that as it may, this renowned artist's dramatic religious paintings, perceptive portraits, allegorical and classical subjects, and radiant, lubricious nudes were still coveted by popes, kings, and by all who could be counted among the noble, rich, and powerful.

Throughout Titian's long career, in his earliest as well as his last work, his paintings have a unique sensuous immediacy, a depth of rendering and color that draws us in, whether the subject is religious or secular. He lived in a world where it was accepted that the divine was always operating close beneath the surface of things, so it is perhaps understandable that even at his most luxurious and sensual, Titian's work seems to hint at meanings that remain elusive. As Erwin Panofsky said about Titian's more overtly allegorical paintings: "we are invited, but not forced to look for an abstract and general significance behind the concrete and particular spectacle that enchants our eyes…"[7] Indeed, it is reasonable to infer that a great deal of Titian's imagination was allegorical and not just in those paintings so clearly if mysteriously symbolic as the *Allegory of Time* with its three ages of man; old looking left, maturity looking forward, youth looking to the right, each surmounting an animal head. All his works seem pregnant with many layers of meanings even if we can rarely know their specific intent.

Around 1561, when the painter was at least eighty, Titian changed his style dramatically. He discovered a new way of seeing and rendering patterns in the visible world. As Vasari, not one of his greatest admirers, put it: "His early works are executed with a certain finesse and incredible diligence so that they may be examined from close up as well as from a distance; the last pictures are executed with broad bold strokes, blobs and smudges, so that from nearby nothing can be seen, whereas from a distance they seem perfect."[8]

Titian had been most adept at courting patrons while running a highly profitable studio. And although artists at this time had only slightly more status than craftsmen, he had attained an unimaginable level of prestige, prosperity, and international fame. Even if Titian's new technique prompted occasional charges of sloppiness, declining skill, and, because this method supposedly allowed him to paint more pictures rapidly, insatiable greed, his reputation remained generally untarnished.

And we know how his new style of painting was achieved. Palma Giovanni who saw Titian work in his later years described how the remarkable surfaces of his paintings were created:

[He] blocked in his pictures with a mass of colors, which served as a bed or foundation for what he wished to express, and upon which he would then build. I, myself have seen such underpainting, vigorously applied with a loaded brush, of pure red ochre, which would then serve as a middle ground; then with a stroke of white lead, with the same brush then dipped in red, black, or yellow, he created the light and dark areas of the relief effect. And in this way with four strokes of the brush he was able to suggest a magnificent figure.... After having thus established this crucial foundation, he turned the pictures to the wall and left them there, without looking at them for several months. When he later returned to them, he scrutinized them as though they were his mortal enemies, in order to discover any faults; and if he did find anything that did not accord with his intentions, like a surgeon treating a patient, he would remove some swelling or excess flesh, set an arm if the bone were out of joint, or adjust a foot if it were misshapen, without the slightest pity for the victim. By thus operating on and re-forming these figures, he brought them to the highest degree of perfection... and then, while that picture was drying, he turned to another. And he gradually covered with living flesh those bare bones, going over them repeatedly until all they lacked was breath itself.... For the final touches he would blend the transitions from highlights to halftones with his fingers, blending one tint with another, or with a smear of his finger he would apply a dark accent in some corner to strengthen it, or with a dab of red, like a drop of blood, he would enliven some surface — in this way bringing his animated figures to completion.... In the final stages he painted more with his fingers than with the brush.[9]

Part of what is revolutionary here, as Vasari saw, is that, when viewed close-up, Titian's new mode of painting calls attention to the paint and the rough canvas which Titian was unique in using. He is making the material elements of the picture and his manipulation of them blatantly obvious. Titian is now revealing himself, the artist in the act of making, an actor in his own work. So, while in Bellini's or Titian's early work, the artist disappears in the painting, in this later work, Titian now is clearly present. The paintings from Titian's old age are overt extensions of himself. The allegorical elements have merged with the personal. Titian's vision is here inseparable from his labor, his skill, his movements, and gestures; these late canvases often bear the marks of his fingers. He has broken down the transparent visual surface of the picture plane and revealed himself, the creator inside. When one steps back, all these elements of material substance and personal presence vanish into a focused play of colors, shadows, light, and darkness and, as if by magic, the subject of the painting appears. The final image and the artist's actions as a living being are simultaneously apparent. This was the discovery of Titian's old age.

Two paintings which Titian made in the last years of his life seem especially daring, original, and personal: *The Flaying of Marsyas* and his last version of *The Pietà*.

Marsyas was a satyr who prided himself on his skill at playing the *aulos* or double pipe. Recklessly, he challenged Apollo, god of the sun and music, to a contest of musical skill. The muses judged, as each performed, and found the god superior. Apollo made his victory final, punishing the satyr by having him tied him to a tree and flayed alive. It is a hideous scene.

Titian's *Flaying of Marsyas* is modelled on a painting by Giulio Romano but is far more extreme in its intensity of expression. The density of paint which Titian applied — modern technical analysis has revealed that there are more than thirty layers — conveys a feeling of writhing torment radiating through the whole painting. The onlookers seem to feign indifference as the calm blond god slices away the skin of the faunlike Marsyas, but pain vibrates in the blood reds, purples, and humid browns of the picture's congealed surface. It is as if the paint is itself the flayed, still living flesh. The muscles, veins, and organs hidden beneath the skin are revealed, still alive. The witnesses do not doubt that this is the fate which a god may inflict on any lesser being, even one of great artistic skill, who does not know the limits of his station in the order of things. Certainly Titian, before whom emperors, kings, and popes had taken the poses he requested, might have had a unique understanding of this temptation and the risks involved in having prodigious talent.

Four centuries later, this vision still exerts its terrible power, and the great Polish poet Zbigniew Herbert wrote of what may have been its fatal legacy:

the victor departs
wondering
out of Marsyas' howling
there will not some day arise
a new kind
of art [...]

suddenly
at his feet
falls a petrified nightingale[10]

In his final painting of *The Pietà*, Titian used the same techniques but to a very different effect. He made this painting while
the plague was still raging in Venice and almost a third of the
populace was stricken. It's dark, smokey, half-lit atmosphere is
redolent with anguish and confusion. Titian made this last mas-
terpiece to be placed over his own tomb in the basilica of Santa
Maria della Gloriosa dei Frari. It was a donation in lieu of pay-
ment for the right to be buried in that church and the work with
which he wished to memorialize his death.

Christ, Mary, and an aged penitent are isolated in the center
of the picture within an aura of rapt stillness in the same way
that all who have ever suffered a great loss feel, for a time, separate from the busy concerns of the living. Behind them is a shallow apse of pale marble. On either side, on plinths carved with
lions' faces are, to the left, a statue of Moses and, to the right,
the Hellespontine Sibyl, said to have prophesied Christ's birth
and crucifixion. An angel flying upward near the Sybil carries a
torch illuminating the figures below. The center however is free
from the kinds of allegorical details that appear in the rest of the
picture.

There, to the left, Mary Magdalene has turned to flee the scene
of the Savior's dead body, leaving the painting's three focal figures. At the center is Christ, whose lifeless corpse has an almost
phosphorescent glow. Mary, who does not turn from the sorrow
she must bear, holds her dead son on her lap. To the right, an
old man, who resembles both Saint Jerome and Titian himself,
makes his way on hands and knees to touch Christ's left hand
and to gaze into the Savior's face. No doubt, throughout his life,
Titian had seen the faces of many corpses; he had also visualized
and depicted the face of Christ innumerable times. Here, as if
these memories and imaginings were conjoined, the old man
projects an urgency finally to look directly at the mysteries of
death, forgiveness, and redemption. As John Steer put it: "The

forms emerge like wraiths out of the circumambient darkness, and mass is reduced to a flickering pattern of colour and light."[11] But color and light in Titian's last work are the direct expression of a world where life force and the inner soul exceeded the bounds of the merely physical or allegorically conceptual.

Titian made quite sure that this painting would be placed in a chapel to the right of the main altar where it remained until 1814. It was clearly his intention that the sight line extending with the Saint Jerome/self-portrait's gaze would reach across the nave of the Frari Church to the altarpiece, *The Assumption of the Virgin Mary into Heaven* which Titian had finished in 1518. This placement insured that long after Titian's death, the old man he portrayed would never cease seeking the Virgin's enduring mercy, and that the reality of Titian's devotion would always permeate the space of the church.

In his late eighties, the revered art connoisseur and advisor to American collectors, Bernard Berenson said of this kind of implicit geometry: "Of course one must learn the language as one learns Latin even if one's mother tongue is a Romance language. [… T]hen it is intelligible."[12] Unfortunately, such understanding won't help us now. The picture was moved long ago and hangs on the walls of the Academia along with many other Venetian masterpieces, their worth established by secular scholarship and popular acclaim.

* * *

Everyone's body is finally, as we all know, a terminal situation, a set of inescapable limits. We fear pain but cannot reliably avoid it. We yearn for joy and security, but do not know how to attain them in any lasting way. Our inner anatomy is known to us via new pains. We know we will all sicken, age, and die. We are subject to illnesses that restrict our pleasures and interests but, if healing means we will be as we were before, we cannot be healed. Bones shatter from minor falls; we realize that our bodies are now fragile. There are pains that can never be resolved and injuries that can never be repaired. There are lethal illnesses, cancers, and others that may be arrested only after painful treatment. But they return.

There is no longer any choice but to let the pain touch, even grip us. We can no longer pull away. Pain interrupts or intersects the continuity of existing we have known before. Pain cracks the surface, fractures what we have assumed, and shows behind, a universe of utter indifference. Pain becomes like heat or cold or silence or ambient noise, itself the environment of continuing, of being alive.

Life contracts around us. The sicknesses that now afflict us are signposts on the way to our demise. Diminishing strength, dullness in the senses, stiffness in body and slowness in mind, these mark a weakening, a loss of reference points to which our awareness, our existing is linked. Our hold on being in the world becomes attenuated. The world is not holding on to us, but is becoming less accessible, more difficult, more demanding. We can no longer impose ourselves. But it is also more subtly communicative as we, the viewers, listeners, knowers, are fading from its grasp. We are momentary, evanescent, and now the world's appeal is more poignant, more worthy of our care.

Earlier in our lives, the direction of things was different. As children, we only knew one world and we wanted things; we tried to understand what works here. In puberty, desires took over with a striving for sex, love, knowledge, strength, skills. These became the mirror in which we looked at ourselves and the outer world. Then we were young women and men, adults, then people in older middle age. We entered the torrent of desires, ambitions, goals that demanded to be fulfilled. The world existed to be reached for, shaped, and held. Desires burned in our bodies, so ardent to make this so. We strained and reached out to grasp, possess, and convey the world.

I remember when I was a baby, standing in the crib, looking into the dim evening light. And feeling the world, the room, something beyond, all vibrating slightly as if waiting. But secretly searching, directing the core of myself out, out of this into the night sky. And failing to find something I could hold. And there is some kind of love breaking apart. Always falling.

Later, as a child, more tentative, a feeling of rooms, spaces permitted, not permitted, filled with the scents and possession of my mother, father, sister. I did not understand these things and I was afraid to be caught exploring them. From my playpen outside, I remember the towering sky palaces of white foamy clouds in the clear blue sky. And then, to school, other children, and the beginning of feeling that to be among others involved learning, playing, acting.

And this relation to uncertainty was a vector, a necessary way of being, that intensified and became all-encompassing. Feeling the infant identity, the child identity, the adolescent identity, the young man identity, the middle age identity, and now the middle of old. The child disappears, becomes a youth who disappears, becomes an adult who again vanishes when inevitably, surprisingly, he or she becomes old.

Now we watch the body age and decay and the world around us change. Then we must find our way in an unsought reality of which an ancient Welsh bard so bluntly sang:

> I'm old, bent in three, I'm fitful, witless.
> I'm simple, I'm boorish.
> Those who loved me love me not.
> […], no one comes to see me.
> […] alas, death will not visit me.
> No sleep, no joy visit me […]
> I'm a cross carcass now I'm old.[13]

* * *

JEAN RHYS (1890–1966)

No one found old age and the loss of physical allure more claustrophobic and hateful than Jean Rhys. She had always known there was nowhere she fit in, but her beauty had been her passport. Aging intensified her isolation and longing. She did not think about being a writer of world importance, though she might have liked it, particularly the money, and possibly the respect. But world importance? She would have seen through that. Nonetheless, she wrote three or four superb books, and, in her very last years, an extraordinary one.

She was born Ella Williams, in 1890 on the sultry Caribbean island of Dominica. Her father was Welsh, a medical doctor, and her mother, Scottish Creole. They were not sympathetic parents. As a child, she received a doll she didn't care for and complained to her mother. "Nothing is fair," she was told. She smashed the doll to bits. She was pleased with her own wickedness. "I can't imagine what will become of you," her mother remarked.[14] She was traumatized when she was twelve and a friend of her father's molested her. She told her parents what had been done to her. They sent her off to a cold and inhospitable English boarding school where she pined for the far-off, bright, and somnolent tropics. She barely got through school. She tried to be an actress, ended up a chorus girl, the mistress and then the wife of marginal men, worked hard at writing, ended up the lover of her editor, of his friends, of crooks; she drifted on the edge of squalor, became, in all but name, a prostitute.

She changed her name to Jean Rhys. She was uniquely placed to know the polluted and cruel shallows which characterized the moral life of twentieth-century England. Her way of writing was clear-eyed, subtle, succinct, remorseless, and uniquely beautiful in its unflinching way. Her books were autobiographical and found good publishers; readers found them seductive and uncomfortable in equal measure.

Jean Rhys was a very difficult person. She found no peace or ease within herself. She wanted to be loved, but, for her, it was a trap. She would accept being manipulated and subservient, but she recoiled if she thought she was being judged or condescended to. She wanted to be a good mother but was unwilling to give her daughter much time. She couldn't bear getting old and losing her looks. She was a violent drunk and created innumerable horrifying scenes public and private. She and her husbands fought, hit, and bit each other. She lived most of her life in poverty, inhabiting grim, sordid places where she created drunken brawls with aggrieved neighbors. Only writing provided her with any focus, and she was unafraid and unashamed to use the innumerable grotesque, humiliating disasters she created or endured in her fiction. She saw through everyone and everything. Even those who wished to befriend and help her, she eventually savaged and sent running. Between 1928 and 1939, she published four novels, all depicting different times in her life, and all describing women used and abandoned by men, unable to find any stable place in the urban landscapes into which they'd been thrown. When World War II broke out, there was no further interest in her work. She moved to a small town in Cornwall with her husband, a convicted conman, and for all intents and purposes, she disappeared for the next sixteen years.

In 1939, Rhys happened to read *Jane Eyre*. The world of books was a realm where she was secure. Now she discovered the book she felt fated to write. This was the story of the first Mrs. Rochester, a half-Creole young woman, abandoned, brought to England from the Caribbean, driven mad, locked in the attic, finally impelled to burn her prison/house down. It was, as Rhys recognized "a marvelous idea." In writing in the persona of existing literary characters, she could bring the anguish of her life into a stable terrain free from the chaotic contingencies of her haphazard existence. The world of literature had provided her with a clear mirror in which to see and present the world she understood so clearly.[15]

The years of obscurity in which she worked almost single-mindedly on this book were more chaotic, violent, and crazy than any before. One husband died under what some thought suspicious circumstances. Another husband went to jail, came home, was sickly, died. She was arrested for being drunk and disorderly. Sometimes she wrote about these things, but she spent almost all the time from her fifties until she was seventy-six, working on the book that would be called *Wide Sargasso Sea*. It is as if this extraordinary book had always lived inside her and had to work its way out. Every word in it has the authority of something lived, imagined, but now finds a lasting place outside both.

A short excerpt may give some idea of how this sounds. Here is the young Creole wife, explaining some of her early life to her new husband:

"I know that after your father died, your mother was very lonely and unhappy" [he encourages]. "And very poor," she said. "Don't forget that. For five years. Isn't it quick to say. And isn't it long to live. And lonely. She was so lonely that she grew away from other people. That happens. That happened to me too, but it was easier for me because I hardly remembered anything else. For her it was strange and frightening. And then she was so lovely. I used to think that every time she looked in the glass she must have hoped and pretended. I pretended too. Different things of course. You can pretend for a long time, but one day it all falls away and you are alone."[16]

Jean Rhys was still alone herself when, very late in life success from this book had come to her and she was established, she gave an interview. She told the interviewer: "When I was excited about life, I didn't want to write about life at all [...]. If I had my life all over again and could choose, I'd rather be happy than write."[17]

Here, ever clear-eyed, she tells us that there is nothing in making such a work that has compensated her for the sorrow, abandonment, and suffering of existence and of getting old.

* * *

Old, then, we must recognize that the body has become subtly and then overtly unfamiliar. It is not a reference point we recognize. We pass by a store window and there is the faded image of an old person, white-haired, tipped forward, shuffling slightly. I do not immediately recognize myself. And the pains are new. Our sense of balance is not quite what we may have assumed. Not that we're dizzy or constantly on the verge of falling. That may well happen later. Rather, it's as if the world beneath our feet is shifting slightly and we lean forward in anticipation of a wave-like movement beneath us. And this instability is felt within. The stomach is doubtful, the heart pauses. Before our eyes, what we look at suddenly clicks to the right, then back. We twitch, recoil at a shadow, almost fall. Inwardly our nerves vibrate, our heart flutters, our hands accidentally let go of things. We inhabit a framework increasingly foreign.

Old, we no longer know what our body is doing. This body has been the center pivot of awareness and movement, and we have taken it for granted. Now flashes of desynchronization come and go. New instabilities imply new deficits. There are uncertainties about whether we have the strength to stand up decisively, run across the street, lift a box of books, walk very far, stand up on a chair, and hammer a nail. We do not know if we have the wherewithal to live decently or if we will end our days confined in a "facility." We do not know if we will outlive everyone we know. We do not know if we will retain possession of our faculties. It is possible we will lose all sense of who we are and yet be, in some utterly unrecognizable way, alive. There is no time of life when we have less certainty, less security, and less understanding that we can rely on. Of course, we do know that eventually and perhaps quite soon, we shall die. And what is that? In the meantime, we are imprisoned in our body. It is the limit of our world, drawing in around us.

My paralyzed friend, a renowned wit and scholar, was still in love with his crazy wife. He could barely move or speak. She wanted to give a party for him. She was so excited when the guests arrived that she forgot she had left him in his wheelchair in the bedroom facing the wall. He couldn't move.

When we were younger, we busily engaged the world in ways we thought to be to our advantage; now this is no longer quite possible. We have been animated by the prospect of gain; now we are amidst innumerable forms of loss. Frequently young and old alike view old age as a defective version of youth or middle age. This outlook diminishes what we see in the elderly and what we may be capable of as we age. In India and China, old age has always been regarded as a different stage of life. It is its own time, and like those before, it has its own liabilities and its own gifts. In old age, all the elements of life become more fragile. They seem more transparent, their connections less secure. The patterning of experience is a weave of gain and loss, remembering and forgetting. None of the threads are stable. But in their passing interplay, they display a vastness and depth in transitory life and endless change. Old age is the time of life when such things become visible. Aging is a transformation into something completely "other."

When we forget a word, we lose, for a moment, our link with the thing itself. The world is, for an instant, slightly out of reach. And we from afar see the clouds swirling before the wind, trees, in the changes of season, in our moods, in what we recall, in the shifts of light on a colonnade we remember from years ago, the flight of crows, the shifting colors of the mountainside, the echoes of a chorus singing in the night. We are seeing something new. It seems that something is whispering to us. And not just outwardly, but inwardly things are shifting. The threads of experience are coming unraveled, each becoming more visible.

Socrates, in Plato's *Symposium*, quoted the Mantinean wise woman, Diotima, who said that every human being continually changes their constituent elements and "is always being renewed, and losing what he had before, whether it's hair, or flesh, or bones, or blood, in fact the whole body." They are renewed, as other parts and aspects are left behind.

> And don't suppose that this is just true in the case of the body; in the case of the soul, too, its traits, habits, opinions, desires, pleasures, pains, fears — none of these things is ever the same in any individual, but some are coming into existence, others passing away. [...] In this way, everything mortal is preserved, not by being absolutely the same, as the divine is, but by virtue of the fact that what is departing and decaying with age leaves behind in us something else new.[18]

We are becoming strangers to ourselves, men and women moving into exile from homes we remember less and less clearly.

We cannot arrest this process. It is hard to accustom ourselves to the reality that the losses we experience as we get old cannot be reversed. Earlier in life, jobs, homes, spouses, and homeland could be changed. Unsatisfactory circumstances could be altered, fixed, and changed, and repaired again. Now the specifics of pain and dissatisfaction will not dissolve. Or, at best, there will be less pain only if there is less movement. Knowing now that comfort will be purchased only by limitations, grief and sorrow are at the edge of everything.

We have this journey in the body. The atoms somehow assemble: their harmony creates pathways; their friction creates energy. Friction and harmony create movement, therefore sound, music, speech. In this way, the assemblage of atoms, coalescing as this body, is a mirror, a world. Because both are in motion, there is time. The chronology of our world and the chronology of our body may appear different, but they are bound together. And it is here that great lusts, great imperatives, unslakable thirsts, omnivorous seductions, furies have appeared, still return, fade, and lose their hold. Even late in life, they continue to return to the stage like actors and actresses before retirement, paler versions of themselves.

Sudden, persistent, intense pain interrupts; it seizes us. An invader without character or personality or history; a commanding occupant, residing in tooth or jaw or brain or back, pelvis, stomach, ear, intestine. Now it is pulsing through our ongoing experience. We cannot move far from it; it pulls us back and becomes the center. We smile or nod or say please and thank you so that it stays hidden in the social world.

And it has no meaning. Everything else: memories, projects, wishes, regrets, pleasures, hatreds become pale. Our life shifts, but the ebb and flow of pain are the critical markers. Pain bleaches out meanings, textures, and nuance within the sensations of our body. It holds our thinking in suspense.

What Elaine Scarry said of torture, is true of pain itself: it is "an undoing of civilization [...], the uncreating of the created contents of consciousness."[19] The grammar of our inner life falters, becomes untwined. We smile, say please and thank you, nod sadly to maintain the faint surface of our social persona, for the world too, losses its power to hold us to its norms.

And then, through drugs or healing, pain weakens, the world returns, and so do we, but we are, for a while anyhow, tentative. And, if we look back to recall even our most terrible pain, we can no longer feel it. There is a tear in the fabric of ourselves.

We see our lives fade, and we fear pain's return. It is as if we are awake but remember a dream, though not exactly what it was. The world of aging unfolds within ordinary conventions and expectations; expands and contracts at the edges. The signals which our senses convey are now less bounded. Each moment expands within itself. Our world has less direction. How things progress, why and to what, are not so assured. We are inhabiting something that shimmers and shifts and is ever more ungraspable. And simultaneously, it is alive with hidden meanings, implications, dangers, and intensities we have before been too preoccupied or afraid to encounter.

* * *

PAUL CÉZANNE (1839–1906)

> Only one emotion is possible for this painter — the feeling of strangeness — and only one lyricism — that of the continual rebirth of existence.
> — Maurice Merleau-Ponty, "Cézanne's Doubt"[20]

Paul Cézanne, throughout his life and in his every painting, strove to find how the visible world is speaking to and through us. He was not looking to find language-like rules, but a way of proceeding so that he could receive and convey the luminous awareness the world unfolds in continuous, momentary, vividly kaleidoscopic ways. Art, for him, was a way of being in the world. Cézanne, particularly in his last years, painted to explore moments of awareness coming to life in the meeting point of what he saw and his seeing itself.

Cézanne was born in 1839 in Aix-en-Provence and forever identified himself with that terrain. There, he studied drawing, but in his early twenties, he went to Paris. This was the center for astonishingly gifted and adventurous artists who were exploring new approaches to optics and painting. Cézanne found himself in a circle that included Pierre-Auguste Renoir, Édouard Manet, Claude Monet, Paul Degas; he was particularly influenced by Camille Pissarro. Although he was accepted in this milieu, he kept himself apart. He made a show of his Provençal origins, and many of his more famous colleagues found him inaccessible, even intimidating. Over the next years, he went back and forth from Provence to Paris, but moved to the Parisian suburbs with his mistress and son when the Prussians invaded Paris in 1870. For the next years, with the support of his doubtful banker–father, he painted continuously. By 1878, Cézanne had attracted the interest of some collectors, dealers, and critics, so he could afford to move with his family back to Provence. Though he often visited Paris, he lived out the rest of his life in the landscapes where he had been born: in L'Estaque, his father's house, in Jas de Bouffan, an apartment in Aix, in Le Tholonet, then in a large studio he had built near Aix where he died in 1906. "I belong to them," he said.

Cézanne referred to his painting as his "studies" and made many versions of the same subjects. He painted forty versions of Mont Sainte-Victoire, many paintings of other nearby landmarks, thirty self-portraits, the same number of his wife, and innumerable still lifes with apples, portraits of his gardener, skulls, many versions of the bathers and so forth. It often took him years to bring a work to a satisfactory level of completion.

Cézanne painted the visual fusion of world and body; for him they were not separable. The senses, particularly sight, mark their junction. He was not concerned with abstraction, with removing all but what might be deemed essential; nor was he concerned with photographic resemblances. He dedicated himself to conveying the experience of the conjunctions of sight and place, or person or object. He worked to present the moments or points of contact where seeing and what is seen cannot be separated. Particularly, in Cézanne's late work, the brush stroke was no longer an element in an ensemble as is the case with impressionistic or pointillistic painting. Each brush stroke did not just embody but actually was the moment where the painter and his world co-emerged. That these marks of color came together as a landscape or still life or portrait seemed, in some ways, almost accidental. They were the outcome of the profound and mysterious harmony of the world of world and senses. This goal, so close, so palpable, was never quite attainable.

> After the terrible heat we've been enduring, a more clement temperature has brought a little calm to our spirits, and not a moment too soon; now it seems to me that I'm seeing better and thinking more clearly about the direction of my studies. Will I reach the goal I've sought so hard and pursued for so long? I hope so, but while it remains unattained, a vague unease persists, which will disappear only once I've reached the harbour, in other words, when I've realized something that develops better than in the past.[21]

In his last decade, Cézanne cut himself off from his former colleagues but was happy to receive visits from younger artists. One of them, Emile Bernard, stayed in a room beneath Cézanne's studio and heard how Cézanne would step close to the canvas, stand there for a minute, execute one or two strokes, stand back, stare, walk around for five or ten minutes, sometimes come downstairs and step outside for a while, before returning to continue with the painting. He repeated this sequence over and over. When he reached a point where he could make no further progress with a painting, he would lean it, face inward, against the wall, so he couldn't see it. He'd take up another canvas right away, sometimes working on one in the morning and another in the afternoon. It could take years for the deeper harmony of a canvas to reveal itself. Thus, there were many pictures in various stages of completion at any given time, even when he died.

He made many paintings of Mont Saint-Victoire, a huge geological outcropping that dominates the landscape around Aix and which had been part of Cézanne's life since childhood. He painted the mountain from different vantage points, in different seasons, at varying times of day; it never ceased to engage him. Late in his life, as his life force became more diffuse, each visual point of contact detached itself from its spatial continuum. Each became, for him, its own moment, its own almost unique sensation, and his brush strokes became increasingly independent, one from the other. In these landscapes of Cézanne's last decade patches of color seem to have their own momentum. In the later paintings, patches of green hover in the sky where a branch extended in earlier paintings. Similarly, fragments of the sky's slate blue flicker in the forest below. Finally, in the last pictures, white unpainted canvas emerges from below. Thus, in his last year, Cézanne wrote:

> Now that I am an old man, about seventy, the sensations of color which produce light give rise to abstractions that prevent me from covering my canvas, and from trying to define the outlines of objects when their points of contact are tenuous and delicate; with the result that my image or picture is incomplete. For another thing, the planes become confused, superimposed [...]. And nature, if consulted, shows us how to achieve this aim. (October 23, 1905)[22]

And indeed, his landscapes of Mont Saint-Victoire became expanses of white with barely connected patches of color to suggest the more tangible landscapes of before.

The philosopher Maurice Merleau-Ponty wrote about Cézanne in a profound and luminous way and said this: "In the water colors of Cézanne's last years, space [...] radiates around planes that cannot be assigned to any place at all," and he pointed to "a superimposing of transparent surfaces," "a flowing movement of planes of color which overlap, advance and retreat."[23]

Cézanne had once described his goal as being to "get to the heart of what is before you." And, to this end, he wished to make his paintings embody "harmony parallel to natural harmony." For "[a] minute in the world's life passes! to paint it in its reality!

and forget everything for that. To become that minute, be the sensitive [photographic] plate, [...] give the image of what we see, forgetting everything that has appeared before our time."[24]

In August of 1960, Merleau-Ponty came to stay near Cézanne's former home and studio at Le Tholonet. During his visit, he walked to Cézanne's studios and hiked through many of the sites which had been so familiar and meant so much to the painter. Merleau-Ponty did not know that he himself would die very soon, and that the essay he was just finishing would be his last finished work. This was an essay called "L'oeil et l'esprit" (The Eye and the Mind), and it concluded:

> If no painting completes painting, if no work is itself ever absolutely completed, still, each creation changes, alters, clarifies, deepens, confirms, exalts, re-creates, or creates by anticipation all the others. If creations are not permanent acquisitions, it is not just that, like all things, they pass away: it is also that they have almost their entire lives before them.[25]

Merleau-Ponty here understood that, especially in old age, Cézanne was determined that his work was an extension of his being in this world and that his every brush stroke marked for others a path into the future.

II

Linkage

> What old age portended [...] was an end to perpetual
> becoming, to thinking that life schemed wonderful changes
> [...]. It portended a blunt break with the past.
> — Ford Madox Ford, "The Lay of the Land"[1]

Aging is not confined to our body. We are inextricably social, so, just as with childhood and maturity, cultural conventions shape our experience of being old. Social norms shape the way others treat us and how we expect to be treated, how we view our possibilities and obligations, and what others expect from us. Old age is, in this sense, a social experience and varies from era to era as well as culture to culture. Now, in the West, as we get old, we find ourselves outsiders.

Over millennia, Chinese have regarded old age as a distinct and valuable stage of life, unique in its accumulation of experience and learning. This outlook, quite common in Asia generally, is unlike that which we now find in the industrialized West. Bit by bit, we, the old, are more isolated amid a social order where once we had some security. Now we look at our world and its past with a more urgent curiosity.

Chinese traditions concerning old age, as Jerome Silbergeld summarized,[2] move between two poles. Confucian principles emphasize filial piety and reverence to elders as the core element in the political, social, and ethical continuity of social structure altogether. Daoist thought and practice emphasize longevity as a mark of having cultivated harmony with the deepest forces in the natural world. Specific kinds of meditation, yoga, diet, and cultural activities such as music, dance, poetry, and painting contributed to extending and enhancing old age.

Painting is a crucial focus in both traditions. In Confucian training, painting is an extension of calligraphy: each stroke reflects the maker's education and personal cultivation. For Daoists, it is inseparable from contemplating, absorbing, and transmitting the innate living power of the natural world. This principle, *kan-lei,* maintains that there is an innate natural responsiveness between things that look alike; this enables depictions of mountains, streams, and so forth, if done without interposing personal propensities, to transmit the life-force of the place itself. Painters, particularly in old age, can achieve in their inner being a freedom from personal biases; their brushwork unites the spirit of place and viewer spontaneously. Great art emerged from such profound inner and outer harmony and was thus both a cause and result of a long life.

Accordingly, when the great painter Zong Bing (375–443) was too old to wander in the mountains, he contented himself with his earlier paintings. He wrote:

> Taking visual responsiveness and mental accord as one's principle, then, given skill at rendering the various types of things [*lei*] [the viewer] will visually respond equally [to the painting as to real landscapes] [...]. Spirits [*shen*] have no boundaries, yet they enter into forms and respond to things according to their various types [*kan-lei*] [...]. If [the painter] is able to depict things exceedingly well, he can truly accomplish this.[3]

In the Confucian outlook that was dominant in later times, painted images were not considered to have this kind of spiritual power. Even so, elderly painters were often acknowledged as having achieved a special freedom from conventional constraints. Fan Kuan (early eleventh century) said: "My predecessor's [Li Cheng's] method consisted of a direct apprehension of things in nature; here am I, learning from a man, which is not the equal of learning from the things themselves. But better than either of these methods is the way of learning from my own heart."[4] Shen Hao said of his predecessor Ni Zan (1301–1374): "[He] could not avoid depending on his predecessors, yet in his old age he followed his own ideas, [...] and was like an old lion, walked alone without a single companion."[5] Guo Ruoxu (1070) said of his elderly contemporary, Xu Daoning: "Early (in his career), he set great store by a meticulous precision; but as an old man he cared only for simplicity and swiftness of drawing."[6] Similarly, Mi Fu (1050–1107) wrote of his near contemporary, Juran: "When old he became bland and lofty in spirit."[7] The great polymath Su Shi (1037–1101) said of Ai Huan (fl. 1068–1085): "The older he grew, the more wonderful his brush-work became. Although it was no longer clear and even, the spirit of it was most uncommon."[8]

"Ah," said David Hockney as he looked at one of Constable's later landscapes, "look how free and fresh. Marvelous." And then he looked again. "You know I told Lucien Freud: 'There's an old Chinese saying, 'Painting is an old man's art.' He liked it, Lucien, and it's true. Old, you're freer. You don't care so much what other people think."[9] But the freedom that Hockney is pointing to here, and which he certainly has taken advantage of, is not mere iconoclasm. It is a freedom to explore patterns that exist outside conventions the artist has, until then, accepted.

Obviously in the industrial capitalist culture of the West, the view of old age developed very differently. Simone de Beauvoir was very clear about this it in her extraordinary book on old age:

Society cares about the individual only in so far as he is profitable. The young know this. Their anxiety as they enter upon social life matches the anguish of the old as they are excluded from it. Between these two ages, the problem is hidden by routine. The young man dreads this machine that is about to seize hold of him [...]; the old man, rejected by it, exhausted and naked, has nothing left but his eyes to weep with. Between youth and age there turns the machine, the crusher of men.[10]

Many might consider this an extreme view, but it will certainly find resonance in the experience of almost anyone over 65 in industrial or post-industrial society. Of course, no society has found an ideal way of caring for the elderly. It is not unique that in many cultures, and regularly in most modern countries, we, the old, cease to be considered full members of the social order. Our economic functions are curtailed, and our dwelling constricted "for their safety"; we can expect to be confined in places where though not dead, we are no longer entirely alive. Without knowing how this happened, we have become — in the eyes of the society of which we were once a part — alien. We are now discarded, even though we may not think of our curiosity finished, our insight depleted, our yearning satisfied, our means of expression exhausted, and our love at its end.

The ground we assumed we would always walk upon is slowly being drawn from beneath our feet. Our steps are, of necessity, tentative. We may act quite confident, but we are not sure where we are going, what it would mean to get there. Groundless. And there is also a kind of giddiness to this as if we were also suddenly weightless.

* * *

RABINDRANATH TAGORE (1861–1941)

Rabindranath Tagore was born in late-nineteenth-century Bengal to a family of immense wealth and power. He moved easily between Indian and Western ways of life and clearly saw the virtues and flaws of each. Much of his writing and teaching was devoted to fostering India's ancient spiritual outlook and making it accessible in the Christian and secular West. However, toward the end of his life, he changed his focus from writing to painting. He believed that visual art would communicate more directly with Westerners. As it turned out, his visual art had more impact in India, where it created the impetus for a tradition of modern painting there.

In 1912 when he was 52, Tagore published *Gitanjali or Song Offerings*. This was a collection of 103 prose poems in his English translations of his own Bengali verses. These are devotional poems that seek to make present the primordial unity within all the world's disparate aspects. This is a goal in much of India's traditional poetry, but Tagore's poems departed from traditional forms and began something very new in his country's literature.

It is the pang of separation that spreads throughout the world and
gives birth to shapes innumerable in the infinite sky.

It is this sorrow of separation that gazes in silence all nights from
star to star and becomes lyric among rustling leaves in rainy darkness
of July.

It is this overspreading pain that deepens into loves and desires, into
sufferings and joy in human homes; and this it is that ever melts and
flows in songs through my poet's heart.[11]

I dive down into the depth of the ocean of forms, hoping to gain the
perfect pearl of the formless.
[…]
And now I am eager to die into the deathless.[12]

From their first printing, these poems struck a deeply responsive chord in the West. William Butler Yeats wrote in his introduction to the collection: "These lyrics — which are in the original, my Indians tell me, full of subtlety of rhythm, of untranslatable delicacies of colour, of metrical invention — display in their thought a world I have dreamed of all my life long."[13]

In 1913, because of this book, Tagore was the first non-European to receive the Nobel Prize. He became famous throughout Europe as the embodiment of Indian culture. Although he had the deepest commitment to India's spiritual tradition, he also had great faith in the West's ideals of social equality. Subsequently, throughout his long life, he worked to harmonize these traditions. This became increasingly difficult after WWI, when British rule in India became more and more brutal as Indian aspirations for independence became more intensely urgent. Although he was always respected, many of his fellow Bengalis considered him too Western in his outlook. Only with his death in 1941 did he become an object of universal admiration and reverence in India.

Nonetheless, for the next twenty-eight years, Tagore continued to develop educational institutions in Bengal, to lecture and perform his songs throughout India and to travel and lecture throughout the world on such topics as the basic unity and intrinsic value of all beings, the importance of art and its power to bring harmony with nature. At the same time, he maintained his prodigious outpouring of literary work. But then, in the last ten years of his life, Tagore changed and devoted himself principally to painting. Perhaps, at this point, he saw that the terrible conflicts, fomented by people with unshakeable convictions, were tearing Indian society apart. Even as the nation seemed poised for independence, the resulting schisms were beyond anything words or deeds could resolve. It was as if he wanted to listen and connect with the wordless where innate spirituality, undistorted by words and opinions, could still offer an enduring refuge. It was a new direction of communication that opened in his old age; it brought to life an ancient promise where the uncertain could open gateways to deeper harmonies. He felt this deeply and intimately. He said:

> The art of painting eludes me like a shy mistress and moves along subtle ways — unbeknown to me. Her ways are such

that I am reminded of what the *Vedas* say: *Ko vedah.* Nobody knows — perhaps not even the creator. Probably in no other scripture do we come across such a voice of doubt — daring even to assert that the Creator himself does not fully know his own creation. It is the tide of creation itself which bears it along in its own current.[14]

My pictures are my versification in lines. If, by chance they are entitled to claim recognition, it must be primarily for some rhythmic significance of form which is ultimate and not for any interpretation of an idea or representation of a fact.[15]

The one thing that is common to all arts is the principal of rhythm which transforms inert materials into living creations [...]. Lines and colors are no carriers of information; they seek their rhythmic incarnation in pictures. Their ultimate purpose is [...] to evolve a harmonious wholeness.[16]

For Tagore, art, in all its aspects, was never a form of self-expression. It was not an exploration of perception nor was it aimed at mimetic representation. He believed that creative imagination was a spontaneous meeting with primordial consciousness, a moment in which the contingent and the absolute showed themselves inseparable. Tagore's artistic search to find and convey the deepest spiritual yearning turned from words and music to explore the silence of painting, a silence beyond controversy and sectarian conflict.

The figures in Tagore's paintings appear in impenetrable stillness, wrapped in a solemn intensity of yearning. Throughout his later life, he made many pictures of imaginary birds, fanciful intermediaries of earth and sky. One of Tagore's earliest ink drawings is an almost archaic kind of geometrical rendering of a shore bird in profile. Its legs extend as two sides of a triangle. These support a body shaped like an orchid; a long beak curves elegantly outward, a round black eye at the center of the head stares blankly at us. A later drawing, angular as a lightning bolt, may represent a crane or long-beaked raptor within whose body hides a man, a rider, flying through space, part of the bird's outer form. Later still, when Tagore added colored inks and watercolors, he painted a dark bird encompassing almost all the pictorial space; it is dark as night sky, but its breast is brilliant orange like the setting sun. And in yet a later painting, a huge, crested bird, its back dark as night, its breast brown and mottled like soil seems to cover the bright green forest into which it flies.

In this kind of landscape, Tagore frequently painted shadowy gatherings of men and women coming together on the forest's edge or wandering beside a village. His cityscapes were less frequent and often rigorously geometric. But he was most often inspired to paint portraits of women who convey a subdued longing. Then, in his self-portraits in pencil made near the end of his life, he appears as an austere figure emerging from the winds, and in a still later picture, he shows himself dissolving into the colors of forests and dawn.

Tagore is not just showing images of dream and desire that persist in the consciousness of an old man. He is inviting us to sit with him in the world of stillness which has opened to him in his old age and to join him in its love, and its primordial harmony. He shares with us a glimpse of the places and moments from which the cosmos emerges and where there is peace. This was the offering of his last years and was respected for the perspective which his old age provided. As he wrote:

> [N]obody has the final reply to the ultimate question. We have a better knowledge of literature, relatively. That is because the vehicle of literature is language which again is dependent on meaning. But lines and colours have no voice. Interrogated, they silently point out their finger to the picture itself. "Look, see for yourself and ask no questions" — they seem to say.[17]

> In perfect rhythm, the art-form becomes like the stars which in their seeming stillness, are never still, like a motionless flame, that is nothing but movement. A great picture is always speaking.[18]

And thus life, which is an incessant explosion of freedom, finds its metre in a continual falling back in death, every day is a death, every moment even.[19]

* * *

About becoming old, Simone de Beauvoir observed:

> We must assume a reality that is certainly ourselves, although it reaches us from the outside and we cannot grasp it. There is an insoluble contradiction between the obvious clarity of the inward feeling that guarantees our unchanging quality and the objective quality of our transformation. All we can do is waver from one to the others, never managing to hold them both firmly together.[20]

We are, when we begin to become an old person, unprepared for the ways in which the world outside is changing us. We are unaware of how newly sensitive we are to the ways we are seen. The young ones look at us, the old, with a flicker of horror they try quickly to mask. "How they have aged," they are thinking.

We know that we are no longer entirely independent. More than before we must look to the world around us for support. We no longer function independently. To walk, we want a handrail. To rise, we need to lean on things. We no longer have the certain strength to walk where we need to go. We find it burdensome to clean our dwellings, wash our clothes.

Others come to play a more essential part in our continuing. We pay people and hope they will not take advantage of us. But we are almost helpless now. We are welded into our outer circumstances which we cannot do much to change. Surprisingly, we find that in this state we so long feared, there is no room to be afraid. Even the claustrophobia is less intense than we anticipated. Discomfort, pain, yes. We are moving within a much smaller compass, and our mind continues seeking. Our gratitude for all who still love us and care for us is desperately overwhelming.

None of us has imagined themself this way. When we were children, of course we imagined being grownups; when adolescents, we wanted to be adults; when adult we may even have imagined having the greater authority of elders. But no one ever had a goal being old. When those who are younger look at those who are old, they see a strange, different, and slightly repellent species. It is difficult for both those younger as well as our contemporaries to imagine how we looked when we were young. And how deformed we now appear, in our pale, wrinkled, cumbersome bodies that move so strangely, with blotchy skin and strange sores, beginning to resemble the corpses we shall be. We are close to the dead, not just in our futures but in our pasts. We are the vestiges of a world the young have heard about but do not know. While very interesting, it is all no longer exactly relevant.

This view of the old is not modern. Long ago, Aristotle characterized the aged as "past their prime", "credulous," "cynical," "distrustful," "tepid, indecisive," "small minded," "not generous," "cowardly," "too fond of themselves," "shameless," "contemptuous," "lacking confidence." "They live by memory rather than by hope [...].They are continually talking about the past [...]. They do not feel the passions much, and their actions are inspired less by what they do feel than by the love of gain. [...] They guide their lives by reasoning more than by moral feeling."[21]

And this state is only voluntary in the sense that we can end our own lives. If we do not choose to do so, then we must age until we die.

More recently, in his poem "The Old Fools" Philip Larkin put it this way:

> What do they think has happened, the old fools,
> To make them like this? Do they somehow suppose
> It's more grown-up when your mouth hangs open and drools,
> And you keep on pissing yourself, and can't remember
> Who called this morning? Or that, if they only chose,
> They could alter things back to when they danced all night,

Or went to their wedding, or sloped arms some September?
Or do they fancy there's really been no change,
And they've always behaved as if they were crippled or tight,
Or sat through days of thin continuous dreaming
Watching light move? If they don't (and they can't), it's strange:
Why aren't they screaming?[22]

Yes indeed, we are now regarded differently. We don't quite know what to do with it. It may be quite a shock when someone first offers us a seat on public transport, or when people seem a bit too solicitous about our walk to the car. It is sometimes apparent that we are not expected to speak as part of the modern world. We are often taken to be deaf. We are treated with fond indulgence. Our desires are deemed eccentricities. Our love is an embarrassment. Our place in society has changed, and no one, neither those who are being nice to us, nor we who are now the recipients of forbearant interest know how to respond appropriately. "It must be wonderful to have such memories," said a young friend, as if the game was over.

A cool, bright Sunday morning in a prosperous mountain college town that was once a mining center. The diner is bustling, cheerful. I'm by myself and there's a seat at the end of the counter. I ask a passing waiter if I can sit there; he nods. The air smells of toast and bacon. No one notices me sitting there for five minutes. I wave down the waitress. She's busy talking to other customers but finally comes over, takes my order, and brings the food but no silverware. No problem. I use the coffee spoon for everything and set to reading the paper. This is something I've always liked but haven't done for a long time: Sunday Breakfast and Sunday Papers. People are happy. In an odd way, I feel entirely invisible, and, with that, a simple contentment. And it turns out, I am invisible. No one sees me at all. Neither customers nor staff. A familiar setting is rendered vaguely foreign. This affords a strange spaciousness, and, with that, the kind of freedom passing ghosts must feel.

Only when I stand in front of the register with a short line of other customers behind me does it seem I come into focus. I give a good tip. It says in the *Yijing* that wanderers must always observe decorum in foreign lands. Just so for the aged visitor.

A day later, I am in a migrant neighborhood in Denver looking for a coffee shop. Everything that might work is closed, but I see, next to a Russian bookstore, also closed, a restaurant with no identification beyond the name of the street. I walk across two parking lots and, after a second's hesitation, push through the brown wooden door. The place is dim, plain, and has a pleasant, heavy atmosphere. It is almost empty, but congenial. There are two elderly couples seated in booths along the wall and a corner table with three men in their sixties. "Hi, Hon," says a short middle-aged waitress. "Sit wherever you like." "Can I just have coffee and dessert?" "Sure. Here's a menu." Home-made rice pudding, home-made egg custard, home-made baklava. I stay. It is a place of settled comforts. Quiet, warm. The few customers who enter are all old. One man with a walker has a baseball cap that identifies him as a WWII veteran. He's alert. I do the math: he must be about 93. The waitress takes her time making sure they order something they'll like. When I leave, the vet's slightly younger companion smiles at me and asks how I am. "Fine, thank you, and you?" "It's wonderful here," she says. It would never have occurred to me to seek, much less find such strange refuge. Of course, we, the old, now have more in common with one another than we did when younger. We are now more inclined to extend, even to aged strangers, a certain tenderness. We all look more alike, more faded, creaky, but know a real gratitude for the time that is allowing us to share this moment in passing. There is a certain intensity to be discovered here, and a new shared loneliness.

"Yes," said my friend as we sat in autumn by a leaf-choked brook, "Yes, there is the physical pain, the slowing down, the medical problems, but the hardest thing for me is seeing my wife get old." He shrugged as he described the persistent slips of memory, the new unsteadiness in gait, the repeated conversations, the kitchen utensils left all over. To point these things out, he understood, would only cause resentment, even panic, and so, living with someone becoming slightly unrecognizable, knowing where this might lead, the need to take care in that eventuality, he was becoming newly alone. And always there are yearnings that will never leave.

William Butler Yeats, very near the end of his life, wrote:

I must lie down where all the ladders start
In the foul rag and bone shop of the heart.[23]

And so, it all changes. Yeats saw clearly the strange intensity that burns like a hot ember in the ashes of our wreckage. It has a different quality and tone from earlier kinds of desire or inspiration. Knowing that not just we ourselves but everything is changing unrecognizably, will end and disappear, this gives a sudden urgency amid an unexplored and poorly documented expanse of time and space. Becoming old, we find ourselves castaways on a thinly populated island. The terrain is lush in some places, bleak, mountainous, dry in others. The passions of the aged are notoriously harsh and uncontrolled, but the focus of our desires is more diffuse, more pervasive, more touched by a sense of departing, more inconsistent with social conventions. We must be cautious in displaying our yearning though it is not less fervent. Thus when one feels a closeness to a new acquaintance, there emerges a sudden, immediate, almost rash, willingness to leap in. No time to do otherwise.

* * *

LEOŠ JANÁČEK (1854–1928)

After a few hours of sleep, I suddenly wake up. Whether I open my eyes or look through closed lids, the night is always dark outside. And how everything shimmers, light blue, before my eyes, here in the shapes of tiny stars, there in the glimmering zones of light! I look down into my soul. Innu-

merable notes ring in my ears, in every octave; they have
voices like small faint bells.[24]

Beginning when he was 65, in the last nine years of his life, Leoš
Janáček wrote five extraordinary operas, a haunting song cycle,
a monumental mass, and a considerable number of symphonic
and chamber pieces, all of which have found their place as masterpieces in the classical repertoire. It was an astonishing outpouring, particularly for one so old, and it burst from an unexpected and overwhelming love.

Before then, Janáček had worked hard to establish himself as
an organist and music teacher. He was the cathedral choir director and the founder of an academy for organists in Brno, the
provincial capital of Moravia in Czechoslovakia. At the time of
Janáček's birth, he was part of the Czech minority in this principally German-speaking city, which was then an important hub
in the Austro-Hungarian Empire. He was married, had two children, and his life was divided between the cathedral, the organ
school, and summers spent in the countryside at the village of
Hukvaldy where he'd been born. Especially in the summers, he
traveled throughout Moravia, filling notebooks with transcrip-
tions of folk music, stories, and customs. Out of this came his
unique usage of speech rhythms, repetitions, and intervals from
folk songs as the fundamental elements in his musical composi-
tions.

He and his wife, Zdenka, were important figures in the
vibrant cultural life of the Czech community. His life was a contented one, but he was, according to the memoirs of his house-
keeper, given to occasional depressions and fits of anger. Often,
he said, he was only happy during summer in the countryside.
After the death of his only son, he treated his wife coldly, and
thirteen years later after their daughter died, their relationship
was, from his point of view, though not from hers, a matter of
form.

In 1893, Janáček began making notes for an opera which
would combine his new musical idiom with a story grounded
in Moravian traditions and life. He did not turn to this project

in earnest until 1901, when his deeply loved daughter, Olga, was slowly dying. She was, he later said, the inspiration for the music, and he dedicated the score to her.

This opera, *Jenůfa,* is a complex story of village love, betrayal, desperate child murder, justice, and redemption. It was set in an early version of Janáček's unique musical style. The opera was finally performed in Prague in 1916; it was Janáček's first real success. Max Brod, who had recently brought Kafka into wide renown, heard *Jenůfa* and was overwhelmed. He urged conductors in the German-speaking world to consider performing it and he worked with Janáček on a German translation of the text. Within the decade, *Jenůfa* was performed in Vienna, Berlin, Linz, even New York; this was the beginning of Janáček's international reputation.

In 1917, WWI ended, and with it, the Austro-Hungarian Empire. Czechoslovakia emerged as an independent republic. Czech language, culture, and folk music assumed fresh importance in the new nation's identity. For Janáček, these elements had always been the deep source of his composition, and now Czechoslovakia's independence brought him a wider audience.

At the same time, when he was 63, during a summer visit to the spa at Luhačovice, he met a woman who opened his heart to a torrent of unceasing but unrequited love that lasted the rest of his life. Kamila Stösslová was vibrant, affectionate, shrewd, uncomplicated; she was happily married to an antiques dealer by whom she had two sons. She was perhaps not insensitive to the social and even the business advantages provided by friendship with an eminent composer. Though she genuinely enjoyed Janáček's fervent attentions, she was not in the least interested in a romantic affair, nor was she much interested in music. Stösslová never had any intention of leaving her husband and was content with a platonic friendship. Janáček's unrelenting passion for her continued until his death, even as he maintained the conventional routines of married life. This drove his wife to a suicide attempt in their last years together, but she did not wish to end the marriage either. Nonetheless, it was the intensity of this painful love that drove Janáček into ever wider and deeper domains of feeling, and with that to establish a new musical idiom which became part of his new culture.

> For me, all these horizons blend together. In them I am one, undivided. I am never certain which horizon, in my mind, comes to the fore. From each one, my music took fire.[25]

The first expression of Janáček's disruptive passion was the song cycle, *The Diary of One Who Disappeared*. It tells of a young poet's infatuation with a beautiful gypsy girl whom he follows until finally he vanishes. Janáček told Stösslová: "And that dark gypsy girl in my 'Diary of One Who Vanished,' that was especially you."[26] Obviously, it was Janáček who was the one swept away.

In 1920, the Prague National Opera staged his second opera, *The Excursions of Mr. Brouček to the Moon*. Audiences did not and have not shared Janáček's enthusiasm for this piece, but even while it was being rehearsed, he was at work on a new, more lyrical and tragic opera, *Káťa Kabanová*. This is the story of a tender young woman whose inner life was eroded by a loveless and bleak environment which finally drives her to suicide. As he wrote to Stösslová:

> Look,... a transparent grey-blue mist rises where the fast-flowing stream avoids even the small stones.
> Up it goes. Now the valley disappears in it. It reaches for the slope of the hill. It has already come up to its peak.
> It has shrouded the whole countryside in twilight. You do not know what is being born in it, what it is that moans, that weeps, laments, beseeches.
> All is but mist
> You think:
> this is the thin corn-ear
> this is the mouth that laments
> this is the eye that weeps
> these are the hands being wrung in grief
> this is the heart that aches.

You think you are about to reach the vision, and yet it is still only the damp mist.[27]

Janáček and Stösslová continued seeing each other frequently for all his life; he often shared a house with her and her children for the summer weeks. Still, they never became lovers. His chamber music and his subsequent three operas mirrored shifting and expanding aspects of this unceasing and ever unfulfilled passion. These great operas involve subjects and aims not usually encountered in more conventional lyric dramas.

The Cunning Little Vixen was derived from an illustrated comic series and tells of the life, passions, mischief, and death of a clever and insouciant fox and of her life among other creatures of the animal and insect world as well as her interactions with the forester, his family, and friends. In this extraordinarily original and beautiful opera, all the passions and dramas of life and death are subsumed in the vast rhythms of nature which is conveyed by the lavish splendor and extraordinary variety of Janáček's orchestration. In letters to Stösslová, he wrote:

"My very own Vixen, where did you take your lament from […]. You, motif of the sharp teeth, where have you seen yourself before?"[28]

The next opera, *The Makropoulos Affair,* from a Karel Čapek play, centers on a woman who has lived for centuries and has tired of love and all ties of affection. She is indifferent to the suffering she has caused, and in the end prefers to die by refusing the elixir which has kept her alive. This harsh and hauntingly allusive opera is a restless exploration of the ways in which time itself frustrates, unravels, and exhausts love. To Stösslová, he wrote:

You, my lady in your fur coat as black as if it had been shed by the very moles themselves, it was on you that I modelled the three-hundred-year-old Elian Makropoulos. You must have been surprised that I, a stranger, once greeted you, another stranger. You were right for Elian Makropoulos only because of your icy, beautiful face. These are the secret paths along which the composer's vision staggers. The day is bright now. The mists have dispersed now: you see the dewy grass, the straight stems [...]. The music is consecrated by the weight of life and its breath.[29]

Janáček's final composition was his opera *From the House of the Dead,* derived from Dostoevsky's journal of the same name. He completed it in 1927 when he was 73 but he died before it was performed. This was Janáček's ultimate vision. In *From the House of the Dead:* love or freedom longed for are momentary episodes, stories, bits of drama in a world of harsh imprisonment. Life continues, offering all the dreams, ideals, moments of release, affection, true love, even if this outer structure does not change. The fact of imprisonment and the reality of love are inseparable and inescapable.

> My vision wanted the beat of another heart; laughter and sorrow as clear as daylight, a seductive spark in the eye, the breast heaving with hot desire, the mind as playful as aspen leaves in a sharp wind.
> My vision wanted a mind catching a glimpse of itself in a child's mirror.[30]

In Leoš Janáček, the great and difficult love for which he suffered and for which he made others suffer was a torrential stream that fused music, conflict, and imagery. Love carried him to enter a primordial sound world that was alive with themes that were violently vivid and meanings that remained elusive. That this came to him only in the last decade of his life made it more necessary, more urgent, and more clear. Certainly, he was trapped in his own longing. He understood the profoundly impersonal nature of the forces shaping his life. The world presented him with this great inspiration and allowed him a great outlet; he accepted both completely. Thus, his music explored and still gives us the inner life of an old man with its sharp angles of pain, acute grief, stultifying imprisonment, motiveless cruelty, as well as its explosions of momentary victory and delirious joy. And the context of all these unresolvable intensities, as they rise and fall, live and die, is a vast sensuous universe of sound, the luminous and seething pulse of boundless life.

* * *

When, one by one, our parents, our kin, our friends, all those we have loved, sometimes deeply, sometimes problematically, die, it tears the fabric which has not just sustained us but has been us. It leaves a hole in a reality we have taken for granted. This is a cellular disruption, a rupture in the web of loves and friendships which sustains us, a loss of substance. We are not the same. Something has vanished. We are diminished and heartsore. Of course, we continue. But as we live on, loss is ever more deeply woven into the cloth of our continuing. Our existence comes to feel less like canvas or muslin and more like lace. It has its beauty but is more vulnerable to rough handling and harsh environments.

Today, I went to visit a friend who, most likely, has a terminal illness. He was not home but had been taken to the hospital with a violent and painful attack from an unrelated illness. I walked in the extraordinary garden he had created. The day was bright and very hot. Beneath a huge weeping willow, a pond filled with water lilies. Shining green lily pads cover the water's dark surface. Here and there, stems stretch upward. And then I saw, half-hidden, innumerable lotus blossoms, large and small, white, pink, yellow. This somehow spoke directly of my friend's generosity, quirkiness, determination.

Then, that evening, I was at a dinner where another friend told me of the neurological illness that, as he said, "every year takes away twenty percent of me." He tried not to look concerned. "I do my best, you know." I held his hand and looked out the window. The vibrant peach sky at sunset intensified the clouds of green leaves of the cottonwoods nearby. All hovering, it feels, on the edge of such empty sadness.

Old age is a process in which we experience ourselves as more and more alien, less appealing, even less lovable while simultaneously, everything around us becomes less familiar. We don't know how this happened, but we are caught up in a procession where we all we know, love, care for, believe to be is disappearing as we pass by.

In friendship, especially in new affections amongst us, the old, we observe a kind of tact. We try to be careful not to press on parts of fabric worn thin. We do not dwell on losses. We do not emphasize strengths or boast too much of things going well. Friendship among the old has an intimacy not based on confidences or understanding. It is based on sharing a certain precarious space. We sit together like migratory birds resting on a rotting fence.

The death of our parents was, we understand, an inevitability, but this deepest net of relationships in which we have been born and which has through our lives sustained us is always being torn apart. My father lay on the ground at the airport, dying in front of me, and later my mother died as I held her hand; these left a kind of schism. I felt a sudden isolation. And a responsibility as well. For now, whatever existence remained of them depended on me remembering or carrying forward the influences and impressions they had left.

And then, again unexpectedly, I was aware that I no longer felt woven into a continuum of time past with the many people they had talked about and the many stories they had told me. Of course, I could re-tell the stories I remembered, but they were no longer a link to a living being with her or his own past and fate. They were now just stories, amusing or touching or tragic or odd, and they lived only because they were entertaining or informative, not because they gave any insight into someone anyone knew.

The death of teachers is another kind of disorienting loss. There is no one now who can say that I've used their teachings well, am doing something worthy or paltry, am a credit or a disappointment, tell me I should consider making a change. I think, in this regard, most often of Chögyam Trungpa Rinpoche with whom I studied and practiced Buddhist teachings for seventeen years, and whose teachings are what I still follow and explore. His country, society, and culture were destroyed, his main teachers killed, his family lost. His presence among us was due, as a fellow lama said, to Chairman Mao. So, when he explained to his students: "The bad news is that you are falling without a parachute. The good news is, there's no ground," he was saying something he knew. And now, it seems that this is the simple truth of being old. We think we hold our own, move forward, but really, we are falling through the world.

New friends, new experiences, new places, new interests do not, cannot have the depth and weight of old intimacies. We cannot know, as we do with people we've known for many decades, the extent of inner sorrows they have struggled with, the disappointments they live with, the hopes and passions that keep them going, the things that always give them pleasure, the weaknesses they can't overcome, their many loves, the wisdom they have. And, of course, we ourselves are no longer known in such density and detail.

The world is continuing. But the depth and weight of love or hate or disappointment or joy is not there to hold us so tightly. Our relationship to the world is thinner, more frail. We are not woven quite so strongly into the world. Our strongest sense of events and people now tends more towards our inner concerns and draws away from the outer world. The world we are living in no longer provides us with family reunions; even if we bring the hors d'oeuvres, we are now guests at receptions filled with strangers.

* * *

In old age, looking back at the past is like walking through an empty house. The rooms are still familiar, but the furniture is gone. The tremor of living is gone. There might remain the faint scent of perfume, occasionally cigarettes, spilled whiskey, but those who flirted, ate, and drank are now far away. The people who used to fill this place with life, struggle, laughter, secret tears, illness, hungers, losses, gains, joy, and bitterness, all are gone. I touch my ear the way my father did in his old age. All that remains is a faint light that hovers in the dusty air. Now, many, even most of the people I loved have died.

Now, for us, the old, our hearts extend into a larger space where both the living and the dead co-exist. It is not exactly the present, but not entirely the past. Simultaneously, strangely now, as we grow old, the domain of the senses, particularly sight, smell and sound have a new shimmer and directness.

What we see and hear now occupies a space that is foreshortened. Present occurrences have fewer implications; they are not part of some project or plan or long-hoped-for future. The sound of the clarinet, the scent of leaves unfolding, the watery sun glowing within gathering clouds are not harbingers of what will happen next. Now these appear alone, exerting a muted radiance, and then a pull and link to feelings from childhood, adolescence, even times of travel not so long ago. They offer now a kind of intimacy, a temptation to find refuge in what is no more.

Marcel Proust was 51 when he died, but in his last year he finished *Time Regained,* the finale of *In Search of Lost Time,* his immense exploration of time, love, social ambition, memory, and change. In this last book, he describes the narrator attending a tea party with innumerable characters who have played parts large and small in earlier volumes, but now he finds them all strangely altered.

How often had all these people reappeared before me in the course of their lives, the diverse circumstances of which seemed to present the same individuals always, but in forms and for purposes that were shifting and varied; and the diversity in the points of my life through which the thread of the life of each of these characters had finished by mixing together those that seemed the furthest apart, as if life possessed only a limited number of threads for the execution of the most different patterns [...]. [And all these men and women] whose conjunction had played a part in forming a set of circumstances of such a nature that the circumstances seemed to me to be the complete unity and each individual actor in them merely a constituent part of the larger whole.[31]

It was not merely the outward appearance of these people that made me think of them as people in a dream. In their inward experience of life too, which already when they were young, when they were in love, had been not far from sleep, had now more and more become a dream. They had forgotten even their resentments, their hatreds, [...]. All these dreams together formed the substance of the apparent contradictions of political life, where one saw as colleagues in a government, men who had once accused each other of murder or treason. And this dreamlike existence became as torpid as death in certain old men on the days that followed any day on which they had once chanced to make love.[32]

Now this evening, I happen to go out to a concert in a mountainside park. It is not quite sunset; high purple outcroppings loom behind the cloudy-green cottonwood trees. We are waiting for friends. And then, the stillness of it all. People walking by, leaves waving and whispering, the air hot and fragrant, the mountains darkening, and there is nothing going on. Nothing is continuing. A stillness all engulfing. Still.

* * *

CLAUDE MONET (1840–1926)

The great symbolist poet Stéphane Mallarmé was consumed by his love for impressionist painting and felt deeply linked to the new expanse of sensuous immediacy it opened.

Everywhere the luminous and transparent atmosphere struggles with the figures, the dresses, and the foliage, and seems to take to itself some of their substance and solidity; whilst their contours, consumed by the hidden sun and wasted by space, tremble, melt, and evaporate into the surrounding atmosphere […]. Air reigns supreme and real, as if it held an enchanted life conferred by the witchery of art […] perpetual metamorphosis and its invisible action rendered visible. And how? By this fusion or by this struggle ever continued between surface and space, between color and air.[33]

Claude Monet's paintings were the quintessence of impressionism. Though he was always admired, he did not have much financial success until his mid-forties. Afterward, he was able to paint as he liked and to create the famous garden in Giverny whose continuous changes always inspired him. Painting and making gardens were his true love. Even as his eye problems worsened, this did not limit him. His grand and shimmering paintings still bring us into a subtle world where throughout the day and dusk, light touches and is reflected in flowers, water, trees, leaves, a world where all material phenomena are transformed into color and light. It was Monet's great passion and his art to free innumerable shades, intensities, and colors of light living within the shifting forms of physical existence.

André Dombrowski cites Monet's famous letter lamenting his growing myopia and asserting his determination to deepen his painting of the waterlilies that float on his pond. "I'm getting so slow at my work it makes me despair, but the further I get, the more I see that a lot of work has to be done in order to render what I'm looking for: 'instantaneously,' the 'envelope' above all, the same light spread over everything."[34]

His brush strokes became freer and more expansive, his colors more bold, and what he depicted became even more ethereal and even less physical: water lilies, water itself, shadows, grasses moved weightlessly in the air as if they were clouds suffused with light.

As Kenneth Clark said:

Claude Monet, whose skill in rendering a visual experience has never been surpassed, created his own marvelous and unforeseeable late manner out of infinite pain. He wrote of his watergarden canvases, "in the night I am constantly haunted by what I am trying to realise. I rise broken with fatigue each morning. The coming of dawn gives me courage, but my anxiety returns as soon as I set foot in my studio… Painting is so difficult and torturing. Last autumn I burned six canvases along with the dead leaves in my garden."[35]

Monet's closest and longest lasting friend was the Prime Minster of France, Georges Clemenceau. In their extensive correspondence, Clemenceau was unfailingly supportive and openhearted. Monet, in his letters, confided his doubts about painting, his fears about losing his eyesight, and many other personal matters. On the day when the papers were signed ending World War I, Monet wrote:

> Dear great friend. I am on the eve of finishing two decorative panels that I want to sign on Victory Day, and I have come to ask you to offer them to the State, through your intermediary; it's not much, but it's the only way I can take part in the Victory. […] I admire you and embrace you with all my heart.[36]

Trenches, unexploded shells, rusting barbed wire, bones, shreds of uniforms, pierced helmets, land mines, poisoned soil still covered the fields of northern France. Both men believed, as did many in Europe, that this savage, furious, and meaningless war had not only killed off a generation of young men, but it had marked the end of all that was best in European culture. Clemenceau and Monet wanted the paintings which the artist donated to provide a fresh pathway, as in a garden in full bloom, to restore the life of all who came to see them.

Monet created an array of paintings filled with concentrations of light as they reflect on ripples, tremble in wind-blown leaves, darken in pulsing shade, bring a tumult of life into the silent air. Monet's donation was eventually expanded to include the eight panels, each two yards high and ninety-one yards long, that are arranged in two sky-lit oval rooms. The *Orangerie*, built in Paris to Napoléon's specifications, was rebuilt to house these paintings. These two friends hoped that the people of France, so deeply wounded by the savagery of the great war, might find solace and inner renewal as they gazed on the paintings' glistening surfaces and shifting lights.

This was a sensuous realm whose shimmering luminosity is free from all the constrictions of the solid and mortal world. What Monet saw in his old age was life stripped of cause and effect, search for meanings or even love; instead he gives us the inner quivering of life, radiant and impersonal. He filled two rooms with the stillness of life, radiant, and reborn. Clemenceau made it possible to give to the world this extraordinary gesture of healing. Monet died before it opened. He was 86 years old.

Clemenceau, in an essay written to mark the inauguration of the installation, recalled his friend saying, as they stood before the pictures:

> [While others seek definitions], I simply bend my efforts towards a maximum of appearances in strict correlation with unknown realities [...]. The only thing I have done is to look at what the universe shows me, in order to render witness to it by my brush. [...] [It is the fault of many others] to wish to reduce the world to their own measure, whereas by increasing their knowledge of things, they would increase their knowledge of themselves.[37]

Twenty-two years after Monet's paintings were put on display, Germany conquered France. Hauptmann Ernst Jünger was a highly decorated German officer in the army that now occupied Paris. He was a profoundly ambiguous figure, not a devoted Nazi, but an obedient soldier. He enjoyed the cultural and social life of Paris. He visited museums and libraries and made extensive notes on changing plant life, but his dream life was dark and tormented. He had dissident friends and for that reason the Nazis arranged that his son be killed. After the war, he would continue writing and become a renowned entomologist. He died in 1998 at the age of 103. But in 1944, as it became evident that Germany would face defeat, he wrote in his journal:

> Paris 16 July 1944
> Fate has started his countdown. [...]
>   We called on Monet's daughter-in-law, who gave us the key to his garden. [...] [T]here is magic in this place. [...] Like our eyes, each little pool catches a universe of light. In the large studio in front of a waterlily cycle that Monet began working on when he was seventy-five. Here we can observe the creative rhythm of crystallization and dissolution that brings a spectacular convergence with the blue void and with Rimbaud's primeval azure slime. On one of the great panels, a bundle of blue waterlilies takes shape at the edge of the pure wavering radiance like a tangle of tangible beams of light. Another picture shows only the sky with clouds reflected in the water in a way that makes one dizzy. The eye senses the daring nature of this gesture as well as the powerful visual achievement of the sublime disintegration and its agonies amid the cascading light. The final canvas in the series has been vandalized by knife gashes.[38]

Monet's luminous paintings still line the two large, oval, marble rooms in the Orangerie. They are unique in their intention and in their serene, light-filled beauty. However, they are now quite hard to appreciate. Mobbed by tourists taking selfies, racing not to miss anything before moving on to the next attraction, jostling to get the best pictures of themselves to mark their passage, it is no longer possible to see these miraculous pictures. Now to sit in this extraordinary offering of freedom and light, one is more likely to have the same experience of isolation and aloneness one feels in a subway station at rush hour.

* * *

When I first lived in New York, I was very much alone. I spent my free times, day and night, walking from neighborhood to neighborhood. There were still, at that time, many different cultures in Manhattan: Germans, Dominicans, Ukrainians, Hungarians, Czechs, Hasidim, Cubans, Puerto Ricans, African Americans, wealthy gay people, poor gay people, artists, and many other smaller groupings. Michel de Certeau was speaking for me when he wrote:

> The moving about that the city multiplies and concentrates makes the city itself an immense social experience of lacking a place — an experience that is, to be sure, broken up into countless tiny deportations (displacements and walks), compensated for by the relationships and intersections of these exoduses that intertwine and create an urban fabric [...], a network of residences temporarily appropriated [...], a shuffling among the pretenses of the proper , a universe of rented spaces haunted by a nowhere or by dreamed-of places.[39]

> It is through the opportunity [such places] offer to store up rich silences and wordless stories [...], that local legends [...] permit exits, ways of going out and coming back in, and thus habitable spaces.[40]

> "Memories," [as a friend said to Certeau] "tie us to that place... It's personal, not interesting to anyone else, but after all that's what gives a neighborhood its character." There is no place that is not haunted by many different spirits hidden there in silence, spirits one can "invoke" or not. Haunted places are the only ones people can live in.[41]

I was fortunate that the late 1960s and early '70s were a time of extraordinary exploration and sheer newness. New York had not yet become prohibitively expensive; arts flourished in ways not before imagined. Attending openings, dance and theater and musical performances, I met extraordinary people and got invited to all kinds of parties. Robert Rauschenberg (we talked about growing up needing glasses), Bob Wilson (text), Jasper Johns, John Cage (shoes), Charles Ludlam (macrobiotic food), Meredith Monk (Buddhism), James Rosenquist, Norman Mailer, Mayor Lindsay, James Jones (American women), Italo Calvino, Jorge Luis Borges, Kennedys, Styron, Julian Beck, George Balanchine, James Hillman (Bruckner), and many others less remembered. The world of celebrity had not yet become detached from the world of ordinary enthusiasts. I never knew what I'd see or hear, whom I would meet. And I was quite shy.

At the same time, I met people who brought back great ghosts from earlier times. At a dinner, I sat next to an elderly English woman who said that she had been at Bernard Berenson's bedside when he died, and that he had had "a good death," by which she meant a Catholic one. Several guests evinced skepticism, which she squashed, proclaiming: "I am a very old woman… I knew Henry James." A friend's father spoke of his visits to Ezra Pound in St. Elizabeth's Hospital. I had dinner with Richard Nixon's psychiatrist's brother. I was introduced to John D. Rockefeller, Alan Dulles. Another old lady I met then would mention in passing her friendships with André Gide, Constantin Brâncuși, Ernest Hemingway, Louis Aragon. The poet who introduced us had known C.P. Cavafy, Antonin Artaud, and later collaborated with André Breton. I had lunch with a man who owned superb paintings by Pablo Picasso, Fernand Léger, Piet Mondrian, many of which had been gifts, and who told me how James Joyce had read *Finnigan's Wake* aloud to him over many weeks, and how "we laughed and laughed."

Women and men alive and dead, sought and unsought, wound their way into my existence. This atmosphere breathed an ongoing passion, a world of possibility, a continuing vibrant life force. There was an organic continuum between past and present, the old and the new. Now, of course, mentioning such names is merely name-dropping. Some are no longer part of the current scene or exist only in college curricula. Thus, the still evolving, adventurous, and expanding world I tried to enter no longer exists in today's much more commercial and institutional culture. These worlds I encountered and wanted to know and extend in are gone. Somebody's memories of something.

And if I think, for instance, of my father's world, the dynamics are the same. When he was young, newspapers were the only mass media; soon there was radio, but television appeared only when he was about 45. He could never have imagined that people throughout the world would walk the streets obliviously while tracking friends and events far away. He did not have a credit card until he was 50, and until then, only a house was bought with borrowed money. The absolute right of profit-making endeavors to exploit their social contexts was not yet established. But by the time he was 60, people's clothes, sense of courtesy, and so forth, had changed. The music he liked, the kinds of entertainment, the kinds of stars and political heroes, had all vanished. He believed that his job and volunteer activities were meaningful and beneficial to others, but eventually he had to retire or resign. After that, he was increasingly isolated. He remained sharp, but his experience was considered by colleagues, whose careers he had supported, irrelevant. Where he had once had influence, he had none. Family and baseball on TV were slight consolations. He died at 78 and his last six years were a silent and almost successful struggle against depression. Now I understand far better the brute impact of the changes he had to adapt to, and I know it was the same for my grandparents (all of whom could remember a world without automobiles) as it is so for me, my siblings, friends, everyone.

None of us ever really imagines that, as we become old, the flow of innumerable small changes in our environment will make us feel ever more foreign. Nearby buildings, even undistinguished and unmemorable ones, are suddenly replaced by yet more anonymous commercial office buildings, apartment houses. Neighborhoods vanish without a trace. It soon becomes impossible to remember what was there before. And the new landscape does not have even casual associations. It has no relationship to anything remembered. The unfamiliar streets do not support our continuity. I don't remember what used to be here or how it felt to walk here. This is a denatured landscape in which I cannot help but feel less embodied, ghostly.

And this ghostliness is composed not just of what happened, but what didn't, an expanse whose range only recently glimpsed: all the lives I didn't enter. Invitations declined, jobs offered and rejected, trips proposed and not taken, dwelling arrangements turned down, seductions evaded, friendships not followed, hints ignored. So, for reasons I no longer remember, I did not accept Douglas Crimp's invitation to meet Charles James, did not go meet Marcel Duchamp, did not go to Nepal or, later, Golok, did not meet Soēn Roshi, or Deshung Rinpoche.

The experience of old age is an experience of incompleteness. It no longer feels, even if projects are finished and desires fulfilled, that they will bring the kind of fullness and satisfaction we might have expected to feel. Perhaps it is because those with the clearest sense of what we were working to achieve have died. Perhaps it is that the world, in general, its culture, its politics, its means of communication, its values have changed. What we do may still be relevant, but it will exist in a context that is quite changed.

Indeed, it is as Maurice Merleau-Ponty, at the end of his own life, wrote about himself:

> [M]y body is made of the same flesh as the world [...], and moreover, this flesh of my body is shared by the world, the world *reflects* it, encroaches upon it and it encroaches upon the world [...]. This also means: my body is not only one perceived among others, it is the [reference for the] measurement of all, *Nullpunkt* [zero point] of all the dimensions of the world.[42]

And now, in this world of total mass media communication, we can't escape this. We know that the blue seas that called to us when we were children are now filled with our toothbrushes, plastic cups and plates, garbage bags. The ocean is not someplace to swim in safely; the whales are dying off; on land, the oryx, the orangutangs, the leopards are almost extinct in the wild. Bison are gone. Elephants are being killed off. Parrots? Spiders? Frogs? All these creatures that give the world its variety and strangeness are being destroyed because we can't stop using plastic, driving cars, etc. Our lives ceaselessly reduce the world that fascinates us into a consumer paradise surrounded by mountain ranges of trash and seas of waste. Just by living, we cannot help making the world a dump.

We, the old, may have betrayed the world with our casual habits, but we are now abandoned in our own time. Whatever patterns of communication, manners, ways of speaking, gestures of respect, kinds of flirtations, courtship, sympathy, all have weakened and are simply called "old school." The new school are those social conventions that appear on television, computer games, and so forth. There was a time when parents conveyed the ways of behaving in the world to their children. This is no longer the case. In a time where fathers and mothers both work, children are taught by the mass media what to aim for, expect, and how to find themselves in the world. The old, in such circumstances, are left far behind.

Now, we "live in networks, webs, and hives, jacked into remote-controlled devices and autonomous apps, moments of being in time, out of time. No longer individual subjects or discrete objects, we have become vibrations, channelers, tweeters and followers."[43]

There is no day we do not learn that our forests are being cut down, our ground water is becoming depleted, our many lakes are drying up; that fish, animals, and birds are becoming extinct, that the temperatures are becoming so hot that much of the world is becoming uninhabitable and that millions of men and women are on the move with more to follow. Soon, they say, many of our great our coastal cities will be swamped. All this, as people of vast wealth isolate themselves, dictators seize land, level cities, destroy cultures. New diseases emerge constantly. Our planetary situation resembles that of the old. For us, the old, extinction is sure and moving toward us. What we experience now is filled with promptings, which link us with all our human past. Here is song from two thousand years ago, by the Chinese poet Cao Zhi, surveying the wreckage of the city where he grew up.

I climb to the ridge of the Pei-mang Hills
And look down on the city of Loyang.
In Loyang how still it is!
Palaces and houses all burnt to ashes,
Walls and fences all broken and gaping,
Thorns and brambles shooting up to the sky.
I do not see the old old-men;
I see only the new young men.
I turn aside for the straight road is lost,
The fields are overgrown and will never be ploughed again.
I have been away such a long time
That I do not know which path is which
How sad and ugly the empty moors are;
A thousand miles without the smoke of a chimney.
I think of our life together all of these years;
My heart is tied with sorrow and I cannot speak.[44]

But, in this exact time, looking inward at our decline suggests something awkward and unforeseen. Our curiosity, our appetites, our conviction that there is more to be tasted, felt, learned, experienced, touched continues. There is a brightness that does not age, a kind of luster, an immediate desire for contact, a desire for love, and a belief that it is all somehow worthwhile. Confronted with the sorrow of loss, the pained confusion of persistent absences, bitterness perhaps, this self-existing expansiveness, this endlessly unrequited love carries us on. At the very least, we will tell this story and sing this song.

III

Waiting

The form on the pillow humming while one sleeps,
The aureole above the humming house...

It can never be satisfied, the mind, never.
— Wallace Stevens, "The Well Dressed Man with a Beard"[1]

We, in our old age, are surprised to find that in some deep and fundamental way our minds are not changed at all. Even from the time we were infants, we have always, somehow, been continuously aware. Aware in waking, aware in dreams, aware in childhood, aware in youth, desire, ambition, lust, anxiety, fear, satisfaction; aware in old age, in loss, in forgetting, in uncertainty, this continuous awareness is almost unnoticeable, unremarkable. It is always here. Bright, clear, impersonal, omnipresent, still; not a thread but the loom on which all our momentary flickerings are weaving together. It's not something or not not something. It's just the fact that we are always looking, hearing, sensing, knowing, seeking, reflecting. So now we find our old age body, our old age world strange, alien because this awareness continues unchanged. Perhaps, because we are less focused on goals, this continuing is vivid if unsought.

As life is drawing toward its end, we are waiting. In old age, a subliminal and wary pause comes to pervade our remembering, our anticipation, our desires. We do not know how to look at, much less prepare for what is ahead. Waiting for death is waiting for what cannot be known, for the moment when even the knower will vanish. We can neither accelerate nor slow down. Underlying uncertainty, fear and curiosity intensify the future, the present, and the past.

* * *

In our old age, the coherence supplied by context becomes unstable, the order received from outside wavers, slips. For example: Sigmund Freud's final essay, "A Disturbance of Memory on the Acropolis," has flickered in and out of my memory, evidence of this ongoing instability. I've occasionally described it to others, and it can still bring me to tears. The essay describes a trip to Greece which Freud took as a young man. Inspired by his classical studies, he longed to see the Acropolis. His father, a practical merchant, objected. It was a waste of time and money; he didn't see the point. Freud and his brother persisted. Afterward, Freud could remember the journey clearly in all its details but, in my recollection, he could never remember seeing the Acropolis. His brother remembered it vividly, so Freud knew he must have seen it.

Freud returned to this moment of forgetting very near the end of his life when he was tormented by a prosthetic jaw he needed since bone cancer had destroyed his natural one. He was living in London with his daughter, Anna. They had been brought there from Vienna by Princess Marie Bonaparte who had ransomed them from the Nazis. His father was long dead, and the cultured world of wealthy and assimilated Jews ravaged and destroyed.

In his essay, he reflected extensively on similar incidents in medical history and literature as he searched for the meaning of this disconcerting experience. Finally, he concluded that he had blocked out seeing this great monument because it would have meant so very little to his father. Freud ends his memoir-analysis saying that he finally understood this forgetting was induced by filial piety. And this was especially poignant to him, as I recalled him writing, now that he was "old, and ill and will travel no more."

I wrote this account based on my memory, but to prepare for this book, I re-read the essay for the first time in decades. It pained me to realize that the specific distortion is not as I had remembered so confidently. Freud did remember seeing the Acropolis, but reacted to the monument by thinking: "So, all this really *does* exist!"[2] He was astounded, on recollection, that he had once doubted such a thing. It was this doubt, this double consciousness involved in simultaneously doubting and not doubting that puzzled him. In his essay, he does attribute this to the kind of filial piety I recall. He ends: 'I myself have grown old and stand in need of forbearance and can travel no more."[3]

For Freud, the original distortion was caused by filial piety, his guilt at persisting in doing something his father found of no value. It expressed the conflict between an orthodox and commercially oriented father and sons who were so enthusiastically assimilating themselves into gentile European classical culture. But Freud found himself returning to what might have been a mere psychological hiccup at a time when history placed it in a tragic and terrible light. Freud's father's hope that, as a Jewish merchant and family man, he could find a haven in Vienna, and Freud and his brother's belief that they could fulfill their aspirations in the secular culture of German-speaking Central Europe had proved to be a monstrous delusion, a murderous trap.

Thus it was that Freud found the subject of this essay interwoven with the memory of his family's and all his friends' and colleagues' aspirations for a world that could never again be imagined much less realized, as his siblings were being slaughtered, relatives scattered, as concentration camps and mass murderers were obliterating the cultural landscape of his youth and subsequent fame. The layered density of Freud's recollection, the methodical way he looked at it, may have allowed him not to be swept away in grief and despair, while finally permitting him to accept that now he was in "need of forbearance."

* * *

PIERRE-ALBERT JOURDAN (1924–1981)

I never knew Pierre-Albert Jourdan, but he was the first person to publish my work. This was in 1969 when a mutual friend, Nicolas Calas, sent him some poems I had written. Pierre-Albert arranged for superb translations and a year later they appeared with Yves Bonnefoy and François Cheng in his wonderful journal, *Porte des Singes*. I was young and callow, living in New York, and did not make the effort I wish I had to be in touch with Pierre-Albert who lived in Paris. Only more than fifty years later did a friend and neighbor give me a volume of Jourdan's work. Now, it is with a kind of rueful admiration that I can return to this remarkable artist who was so long ago so very kind to me. What an extraordinary and courageous man he was.

In the following, written in the countryside during the last days of his life, as mind and body suffered in the final stages of lung cancer, Pierre-Albert's perspective shifted in and out; he sometimes calls himself "you." It was no longer the world of culture or literature that preoccupied him. All such struggles to find and create order slipped away. He looked out the window and the landscape he saw no longer supplied order but a kind of wordless meaning devoid of human ambition. As he wrote:

Hide in a landscape, vanish behind foliage, burrow into a hill.[4]

The eye can roam freely. It feels no pain when pausing to contemplate these faded blues. It does not experience that inner trigger mechanism that locks you up.[5]

Last night, the north wind cooled off the heat and cleared the horizon, At present, it is playing the game you know well: shaping clouds with the aid of Mt. Ventoux. There they are, as if caught in a trap, unable to pass over the ridge and coming apart like an immense soft spinning top. I don't wish to push the similarities any further.

I cannot truly distinguish my own suffering, at least at this bearable stage [...] from that of, for example, these trees assailed by the violence of a wind gone mad, from their own struggle; and from that of animals who are tortured, poisoned, stalked, and hunted down and who are yet, each of them, our sustenance. I refuse to pay the slightest attention to those, their ego bleating at the slightest warning, are surprised to discover that they have not remained at the centre of the world. Suffering extends so far beyond our understanding.[6]

We are settling into a new life (we'll have to find another word), one in which we are so completely uprooted [...] that it could make us weep. And this, moreover, happens often. Everything is perfectly regulated in all ways, nothing to say about that. But you are *excluded*. Those maple trees outside, that sky no longer belong to you. What is this "new life"? It is *separation*.[7]

It is true that we incessantly roam just outside this spaceless space that we never enter, alive. Sometimes it even seems to constitute us. Yet we have this regrettable habit of approaching it from the wrong side: this fear it inspires is perhaps only the fear of being alive [...]. The gentleness of twilight has no name.[8]

How I understand this! Through great rifts in the landscape?[9]

Pierre-Albert Jourdan wrote this assertion of unceasing and unconditioned awareness and this last question about reference point on the eve of his death.

* * *

One morning a few years ago, I was playing Canfield solitaire, and, as always, cheating. I suddenly knew why I was doing this. True, I do find shuffling and dealing relaxing. But the real reason to play is the way the game produces a relationship to observing patterns and participating in their emergence. The order for the cards as they emerge from the newly shuffled deck is, at least in theory, random, chaotic. Then they are then placed in two forms of order: the alternating colors of ranks descending hierarchically from the rulers and the ascending numerical values ascending from the aces. On that morning, I realized that my interest in achieving the specific order which is the goal in the game had waned.

Now I simply wanted to watch patterns develop. In writing, for instance, a momentary insight, a twinge of emotion, a random encounter, when written as part of something larger, will echo and highlight new relationships throughout the entire text. When sentences are moved or cut, unexpected spaces, rhythms, and balances emerge; a new overall form begins to take shape, hinting at meanings and possibilities yet unforeseen. This happens also in reading and, yes, in life.

And with that, I saw how discovering and creating patterns was a deep intrinsic vector in our mind's conscious and perhaps unconscious life. We, the old, see clearly that life has not been created for our convenience or satisfaction. The pattern, articulated in Buddhist texts as birth, old age, sickness, and death, is indeed so. Seeing that simple and inescapable pattern, we realize we are enmeshed in something relentless and more impersonal than we may have recognized, even as we seek to create or live within subsidiary patterns of our own devising. But life is not a normative process. Accepting its larger laws does not assure happiness. Dying, we are moving beyond the boundaries of life and death. We will die quite soon, and now we see the busy pattern-making that surrounds us differently. There really is nothing we can cling to, no raft, no spar, no map.

Moving ahead has been intrinsic to our being. "The mind is that which seeks an object," said the early Buddhists. But now, in old age, there is less and less to grasp. We face the end of moving and doing. We are old and now we must wait. It is strange that now we can accept existing with so little future. We can live without feeling we must constantly go forward. We can live without visualizing what will be next. Patterns swirl by in free-fall.

* * *

Pattern and chaos are the polarities between which we have progressed. This has been so from ancient times. Mencius, the Chinese philosopher who lived in 400 BCE, described the cosmos as originally a wild, dangerous, unlivable state of being, seething, raw, incomprehensible, illogical. The land, the seas and streams, the weather were utterly unstable and unpredictable. The world could not sustain agriculture, social hierarchies, urban settlements, or any other kind of order.

> In the time of Yao, all under Heaven was not yet regulated. Flooding waters flowed throughout, inundating all under Heaven. The grasses and trees flourished, the birds and beasts multiplied, the five grains did not grow, and the birds and beasts pressed in upon man [...]. Yao alone was concerned.[10]

The great China scholar, Michael Puett continues:

> The *Xunzi,* a text from the third century BCE, makes a similar point [...]: "Heaven and Earth gave birth to the superior man. [...] Heaven and Earth have no pattern, ritual and righteousness have no unity; [...]." According to this text, [...] humans must create patterns in the form of a clear hierarchy to guide Heaven and Earth, as well as future humans.[...]. [This and other] texts portray humans providing order to what was previously a chaotic natural world, transforming and domesticating that world so that it now functions as a patterned system: through human organization.[11]

Binding singular entities and events to larger contexts and longer time spans somehow gives pattern and thus meaning to chaos. Pattern and chaos cannot be separated but must be continually distinguished, woven together, and re-woven. And particularly for the Chinese, the most enduring patterns were found in the distant past. Chinese culture likewise accepted that the aged, because of their longer experience and more extensive study, were able to see this most clearly.

Age, change, and loss push all of us to subtler, more transitory, and ever-more capacious kinds of order. This is the deepest vector moving us. We sense the wild and chaotic close by; we know our world is fragile. We know our lives may fall apart at any moment. Our searching and shaping continue; no pattern or structure, organization, or form, whether physical, social, spiritual, or artistic is ever complete or ever remains intact. Chaos, the all-consuming power of disorder, impels us towards patterns hidden in the vastness as well as in the minutiae of the world.

* * *

MARY DELANY (NÉE GRANVILLE) (1700–1788)

Mary Granville's life in its early years was constrained and bleak in ways familiar to most intelligent women trapped in the impoverished English gentry of the time. Daughter of a colonel, niece of minor nobles, she received a fine education in the hopes she would find a position at court. As part of her training, she learned English literature, French, history, dancing, needlework; Handel taught her music. Changes in the royal succession and her family's increasingly precarious finances put an end to such plans. At the age of seventeen, she was forced to marry a 60-year-old wealthy Member of Parliament, Alexander Pendarves. Though Mary could distract herself with riding, sewing, visiting friends, it was her husband's drinking, loss of much of his fortune, and persistent gout that set the tone of their marriage. When, after seven years, he died, she was left with a small pension that was nonetheless adequate to her needs.

"Why," she asked, "must women be driven to the necessity of marrying? a state that should always be a matter of choice! and if a young woman has not fortune sufficient to maintain her in the situation she has been bred to, what can she do, but marry?"[12] Accordingly, she was glad to take advantage of her widowhood and enjoy prolonged visits with many highly placed, wealthy, and learned friends. Her quick intelligence, sensitivity, and inventiveness made her a valued guest at a time when people of means liked to stock their households with interesting visitors. "She was still a friend of Handel, corresponded wittily with Jonathan Swift [...], knew Edmund Burke, was wooed by John Wesley, entertained and was entertained by Garrick, [...] King George III and Queen Charlotte were on terms of intimate friendship with her and brought her comfort and happiness in her last years."[13]

At the same time, her avid scientific interest in the forms and development of plants became deeper and more detailed. On a visit to Dublin, she became friends with Dr. Patrick Delany, famous for his garden and his knowledge of botany. When his wife died three years later, they married. "Their shared pleasure in gardening and his encouragement of her painting, shell-work and needlework resulted in a surge of activity in a variety of media. In all these, the basic theme was the flower."[14] Flowers, with their infinite, delirious generosity of colors, shapes, smells, and transformations, were to this outwardly conventional woman of immense intelligence and sensuous acuity a domain of almost utter freedom.

The Delanys lived together happily for twenty-five years, but, at 68, Mrs. Delany again found herself a widow. Fortunately, her close friend, the Duchess of Portland, then invited her to stay at Bulstrode, her lavish country estate. The two women shared a scholarly interest in plants, and the extensive gardens provided them a great range of plant life to study. They often discussed their detailed observations with visitors who included the most eminent botanists of the time. Even the celebrated scientist Joseph Banks invited them to inspect his personal collection of botanical samples and drawings that he had accumulated while sailing with Captain Cook.

Throughout her life, Mrs. Delany corresponded regularly with friends, relatives, and others in the upper strata of English society. Her letters were observant, warm, spirited, sometimes witty, and they give extensive accounts of luncheons, teas, and dinners, finding servants for friends, expressing concern for others' medical problems, purchasing a carriage, reporting on royal gossip and public events. She noted, for instance, on the splendid opening of the Pantheon, that "To balance these delights the *High Street* robbers give many panicks, but pleasure will conquer all fears."[15] Her scientific interests and, later her artistic concerns rarely appear in these letters.

When she was 72, Mrs. Delany made the discovery that led her to the work that made her famous. The petal of a red geranium fell onto her black ebony desk and landed accidentally beside a piece of red paper of exactly the same shade and color. She began cutting the paper to make a replica of the petal. The Duchess happened by and thought that her friend was dissecting the geranium. Mrs. Delany immediately understood the possibilities of her chance discovery, looked up and remarked. "I have invented a new way of imitating flowers."[16] And, though decoupage had been popular with court ladies for many years, she had discovered a form of collage never seen before. She called her flower portraits, "paper mosaicks," and her method was as follows:

With the plant specimen set before her, she cut minute particles of colored paper to represent the petals, stamens, calyx, leaves, veins, stalk and other parts of the plant, and, using lighter and darker paper to form the shading, she glued them on a black background. By placing one piece of paper upon another she sometimes built up several layers and in a complete picture there might be hundreds of pieces to form one plant. It is thought she first dissected each plant so that she might examine it carefully for accurate portrayal.[17]

With tissue and papers of all hues and shades, Delany was able to spontaneously cut the wafer-thin tissue without any drawings or apparent planning.[18]

In her extraordinarily insightful book, *The Paper Garden*, Molly Peacock reaches something deeper in Mrs. Delany's work. "She was determined to find out the dimensions and names of things. On nearly every flower she would write the Latin name, and often the vernacular name and the place and the date the work was executed. These notations combine elements of botanical labels and the headings of diary entries. They are botany and reflection both."[19] And Peacock continues: "In the dreamlike, luminous atmosphere of memory, imagination and mourning, the flowers have something of the feel of self-portraits as well."[20]

Delany was always investigating and learning from trees, grasses, shrubs, and flowers. She sought out the inner relationships of the elements, structures, and patterns which gave them shape. She transposed the forms she found to a more easily accessible and lasting medium. This was a world where life expanded freely and created unimaginable kinds of sensuous beauty. There was no limit. And so, when she suddenly discovered a way to replicate, pay homage, give thanks, and express the complex pleasures and insights which the plant world had shared with her, she knew what she had found. "An ingenious mind is never too old to learn," she said.[21]

Mrs. Delany herself said that her flower portraits were "to supply the loss of those that had formerly been delightful to me; but had lost their power of pleasing; being deprived of the friend, whose partial approbation was my pride."[22] Using paper cuttings to bring the simulacra of flowers to life produced evocations of people she loved and had lost, feelings and memories that lived in her. These were transposed onto the ephemeral world of flowers, ever changing forms that offered a crossroads, a union of past and present, of what could be said and what could not. This is the refined and complex inwardness of Mrs. Delany's artistic work. She used the structural framework of flowers as the pattern on which to explore the intimate subtleties of her inner life, her past, and ongoing passions. And it pleased her deeply that she had found a way of expressing herself congruent with the new world of scientific discovery. Mrs. Delany's subtle art lives in a unique communicative juncture of the fragile inner structures of flowers, patient skill, and the delicate intensity of her vibrant inner life. Her 985 remaining "paper mosaicks" convey a sensuality, lucidity, and longing far more haunting than what we might otherwise impute to a gentlewoman who had to hone her social skills and sing for her supper without ever seeming to do so.

When Mrs. Delany was 85, the Duchess of Portland died unexpectedly, and the Duchess's heirs made it clear that Mrs. Delany was no longer welcome as their guest. She would have been homeless had not King George III intervened. He gave her a house on the grounds of Windsor Castle and a pension more than ample to support her for the rest of her life. Her eyesight was failing, and she could no longer make her intricate collages. She often taught, however, and she remained a lively conversationalist. Many came to visit her, and she enjoyed the friendship of the King and Queen. Life, in the end, was kind to her.

It might be easy to think that Mrs. Delany's accomplishment was simply the superficial craftsmanship of an idle woman, bored in her privileged setting, playing at science and art. But we do not choose our births; all societies are hierarchical and create innumerable outer and inner constrictions. In such a context, plant life, with its infinite almost delirious generosity of colors, shapes, smells, and transformations, offered themselves to this outwardly conventional woman of immense intelligence, sympathy, sensual awareness, generosity, and passion.

* * *

Old, we can no longer perpetuate our will, our consciousness, our knowing, our spirit. Now, from a greater distance, we see they are constructs which we have inhabited. These terms describing continuity are devices of the living. The framework of such "knowing" is contingent and temporary. But, even in the context of such uncertainty, we can look at our language, logic, ways of life, the patterns that carry us and that we carry. More easily now, as if we were looking at a constellation or listening to a fugue, we see their power, their clarity, their beauty. Certainly, it is a deep part of our nature, that even as we near death, still we are sharing the shapes and directions of our lives in the deepest and most beautiful ways we can.

* * *

STÉPHANE MALLARMÉ (1842–1898)

At the end of his life, as age stripped away other needs and pre-occupations, Stéphane Mallarmé saw the enduring patterns that had moved and shaped his mind and life as if they hovered in a void without boundary. He conceived of a new way to render what he saw with letters of varying sizes inscribed on blank white sheets of paper. There had never been anything before that looked like this and made such demands on the reader. Not only did Mallarmé, despite failing health, labor to write this final poem, but he oversaw every aspect of its layout and printing.

For Mallarmé, the power and radiance of what we perceive lives simultaneously within and outside us. Thus, the goal of his poetry became, as he said: "to convey, not the thing, but the effect it produces."[23] To do so, in each poem he devised strict patterns of vowels, consonants, and accents which would sustain a geometry of images and tropes. Beyond the meanings which the conventions of syntax and definitions provide, he looked to such intricacies of rhythm and assonance to create, within the words and phrases, other connections that hover just beyond language. The transitory nature of the sensual was at the axis of his work.

Though these poems look on the page like conventional sonnets, elegies, and so forth, Mallarmé thought of them as language structures, hollow as a vase or wine glass, each designed to attract and hold a specific breath or atmosphere, to capture the moment of longing, joy, or loss from which the poem took birth. He believed in a deep continuum of language that the randomness of inspiration, change, and destruction could not touch.

Mallarmé's life was marked by material hardship, but he enjoyed the continuous and profound admiration of many writers and artists, amongst them, Édouard Manet, Edgar Degas, James Whistler, Paul Verlaine, Paul Valéry, Claude Debussy, Claude Monet, and Auguste Renoir, all of whom visited him regularly. His discussions about painting, music, poetry, and the arts in general were famous. Through all this time, he was making notes for a project he called *Le livre* (*The Book*). He wrote: "The Book: [I am] convinced that fundamentally there is only one, (which has been) attempted unknowingly by all those who have ever written [...] the Orphic explanation of the Earth, which is the only duty of the poet [...]: the true rhythm of the book, at once impersonal and alive, down to its pagination, is juxtaposed to the equation of this dream, or Ode."[24]

In 1894, he was able to retire from his irksome and exhausting job as a high-school teacher. Though his health was already declining, he finally was able to work on a text that would come closest to fulfilling some of the goals he discussed in his notes for *The Book*. Then, as he neared the end of his life, he struck out in a completely new direction.

Un coup de dés (*A Roll of the Dice*), deployed, in addition to the elements mentioned above, a complex visual pattern that displays hierarchies of meaning in a graphic way. This is a level of abstraction in poetry never explored or seen before. Though the musical quality of his earlier poems remains, the lavish imagery has been stripped away. Here, we enter a directionless white space which is the ground from which emerge whatever patterns of pleasure and understanding come to us. It is the pattern beneath all other patterns in which chance and fate dance together. It is worth noting that the French word for "chance," *hazard* derives from the Persian word for "dice." A cube with markings which, tossed as part of a frivolous amusement, can, as happened in the great Indian epic, the *Mahābhārata,* end up determining the fate of humanity.

The text that follows reproduces (with translation) only the two largest registers of text. The smallest and more voluminous part of the poem is best examined in the printed poem. Mallarmé died before its printing was complete.

UN COUP DE DÉS
A THROW OF THE DICE

JAMAIS
NEVER

SOIT
THOUGH IT BE

LE MAÎTRE
THE MASTER

N'ABOLIRA
WILL ABOLISH

COMME SI
AS IF

COMME SI
AS IF

SI
IF

C'ETAIT   LE NOMBRE
IT WAS   *THE NUMBER*

EXISTÂT-IL
WERE IT TO EXIST

COMMENÇAT- IL ET CESSÂT-IL
WERE IT TO BEGIN AND WERE IT TO END

SE CHIFFRÂT-IL
WERE IT COUNTED

ILLUNINÂT-IL
WERE IT ILLUMINATED

CE SERAIT
IT WOULD BE

LE HASARD
CHANCE

RIEN
NOTHING

N'AURA EU LIEU
WILL HAVE TAKEN PLACE

QUE LE LIEU
ONLY THE PLACE

EXCEPTÉ
EXCEPT

PEUT-ÊTRE
PERHAPS

UNE CONSTELLATION
A CONSTELLATION[25]

What Mallarmé shows in this x-ray-like arrangement of thought in words is that a single decision, a single choice, or gesture is the live seed of a larger structure, of shape or destiny. This does not eliminate the chaos from which it emerged and into which this pattern or life will again dissolve, but in the vector of speaking, noting, telling order, and disorder, existence and non-existence can find momentary accord.

The painter Arakawa once said: "Mallarmé was finally alone… He looked in the mirror and, at the end of his life, saw nothing but a vast array of stars moving slowly in space."[26] But what is so very mysterious here is not just the patterning of words as they move, large and small, to articulate a fleeting emergence in fragments and glittering shards; it is the space of the page that we become so aware of. A clear empty space before us and within us too. And, at the end of his life, how naturally it seemed to come to Mallarmé that words, images, ideas fall through this pure expanse and end, emptied of implication, in a void.

* * *

Waiting, our memory merges with sensation. Our memory is not a thing, not a data bank or library. It flows in us and, like lymph, pervades our body. So, I am looking out the window at cumulus clouds rising over the foothills. And again, seventy-five years before in my playpen in the front yard, I am looking up at the towering white cumulus clouds rising in the motionless blue sky. As I stand there, I can still hear the screech of a car's brakes, a thump, a terrible animal scream. A robin's egg turquoise car hit our dog. She is moaning in the street. My mother runs out. A bald man in a white shirt stands helpless and upset. The dog writhes. My mother calls for help, then stands so I can't see my dying pet. But I do. I still feel the solemnity of being a witness to something final. I remember her lips pulled back; her white teeth wet with her own blood. It was summer. The air was humid; a neighbor had just cut his lawn. Someone here now is cutting the grass.

Streams of consciousness, streams of stories, torrents of moments like a remembered summer wind or a stolen chocolate bar come to the fore as others recede. Sitting in a restaurant, we can simultaneously smell perfume while we're eating shrimp, listening to a mediocre joke, sensing an argument behind us, having a slight cramp in our leg, noticing a waiter look our way, remembering how much my father liked this place. And I can remember all this as an example of random memory. It does not sustain or confirm existing; it is continuing.

Our experience in any moment is the weaving of countless threads. As we live through the day, hundreds of thousands of strands from the present and the past, desires, thoughts, emotions, all interact in constantly varying proportions. As we recognize patterns of coincidence and divergence, it is our pleasure, our control in a situation never quite resolved. Weaving and reweaving as past and present, present and past ripple across our field of awareness.

A breadth of acceptance opens and expands around us as we age. The future wavers. The past is always incomplete, unfinished. Around us, the world evens out, expands. The one who lives inside this aging, this change, looks out, takes it in.

We are waiting. Sometimes we are afraid, more often we are simply not paying attention. But as we move further into old age, a certain objectless clarity opens out within and around us. It is expansive, direct, present. It feels like we are returning to somewhere we left long ago. We are here, and there is nothing that needs to be done, nothing that needs to be considered. It is like sitting in the shade beside a lake on a bright clear day. We are not cut off from what we remember. We have not abandoned the press of making and unmaking. But none of this is so necessary anymore, nor is it really expected. We have no need to engage things further. All these things now move and vibrate around us at a slight remove. Their solidity, their seriousness are now painful.

The body now cannot find ease. Its hungers, needs, heat, and cold are conditions we cannot escape. We cannot stop making plans for continuing, ways to impose a desirable outcome. There is a thin transparent membrane, a kind of sinew that is keeping us in this form and its incessant need to move. The sky and change of day, the clouds drifting over the mountain ridge, a crow landing on a dead branch, a footstep near the door, begin to exhaust whatever sense of significance we think might we need. There is nothing to do now but wait for a deeper and unknown pattern to become visible, an order so immense and devoid of boundaries that it cannot be distinguished from space itself, a self-sentience without object or subject, never before imagined.

The world is moving away. Clouds, mountains, trees, a stream. White, blue, green. A silence.

Every day we look back and we begin again.

Waiting, we look out on the expanse of memory whose shores are less distinct, whose depths seem greater, whose surface is increasingly still. As we are move further into old age, memory is binding us within our body, language, place, time, awareness; now it is less hidden within the purposes of daily life. Patterns flow, extend from past toward future, expand for a moment there, contract. It is our intimacy with worlds, patterns, times that no longer exist. We no longer have a place to live as it extends its own domain.

* * *

ANDREA PALLADIO (1508–1580)

Our species seems always to believe that somewhere in the depths of our historical and personal past, we can find a pathway to order. In Europe, in the sixteenth century, amid the chaos of conflicting dynastic claims and ceaseless murderous warfare, memory found a new frame of reference. The biblical history of the world was augmented and altered by studying texts, art objects, and ruins from the past of classical Greece and Rome. This new past afforded altered vistas in the present landscape and opened new possibilities for exploring and recreating the world. By extending the continuity of Rome's classical past, Andrea Palladio asserted a temporal and spatial cultural coherence amid the dangerous chaotic present. It was a vision where human endeavor could now become paramount. Out of warfare, religious conflicts, blood feuds, and political upheavals, the great serenity of Palladio's art evolved from contemplating the classical past. What he then made in this world offered stability and solace even as it was both dreamlike and real.

Andrea Palladio was born in northern Italy where he was trained from childhood to be a stone mason. His life changed sharply when, in his twenties, he was hired to work on various building projects by the renowned scholar and nobleman Giangiorgio Trissino. Trissino soon recognized the young man's exceptional gifts and invited him to join a company of young aristocrats who devoted themselves to a humanistic curriculum, studying ancient Greek and Roman culture. They called themselves the Accademia Olimpica, and their aim was to make classical Roman literature, rhetoric, music, mathematics, philosophy, civil law, and architecture the basis of sixteenth-century Christian civilization. Palladio was an avid student and quickly absorbed the subjects that became the foundation of his life as an architect. Later, as Trissino's guest, Palladio made three visits to Rome where he became familiar with a large circle of thinkers and artists. He spent much of his time there finding, measuring, and making schematic drawings of all the Roman buildings then known. Later, he would publish a record of these findings, as well as a guidebook to Roman monuments. Soon after, Palladio gained a reputation throughout northern Italy, particularly in Venice and Vicenza, as the most capable and inspired architect of his age.

"Palladio's Humanist training taught him that the supreme and logical order that permeates all God's creations should be 'imitated' or reflected in the creations of humankind."[27] "'The rules of arithmetic,' said Palladio's friend and patron, Daniele Barbaro, "are those which unite Music and Astrology; for proportion is general and universal in all things given to measure, weight and number.'"[28] These systems of numerical proportions were derived from Pythagorean writings on mathematics, music, and cosmology. And as Rudolf Witkower commented, for Palladio "the proportions of sounds and in space were closely related, [...] and of the validity of one and the same harmonic system. These were convictions which belonged to the general intellectual make-up of the Renaissance."[29]

Palladio's designs reflected a deep utopian impulse to return to a way of life in accord with both natural proportions and the primordial principles of the universe. Even at the beginning of his architectural career, Palladio was unique in his ability to apply the numerical ratios of musical intervals throughout the design of an entire structure. In his buildings, the height and width of the exteriors were created with the same proportions as the rooms and open spaces of the interior. His purpose here was not just to work within a contemporary idea of perfect beauty, but to follow his ancient predecessors in creating spaces that were congruent with the natural proportions of the universe. The result was that the residents and their guests could experience the spatial harmony of a supremely ordered world.

At the same time, Palladio's concerns were entirely pragmatic. His study of Roman hydraulics and engineering enabled him to bring his buildings to a new level of practical efficiency and structural coherence. His villas, country residences for noble families, were palatial and utilitarian; they functioned as centers of public social power while accommodating the needs of a large agricultural operation.

In most of Palladio's country villas, the large central third of the building dominates two symmetrical side elements. The noble owner and his family and guests occupied the dominant center, while the buildings on the symmetrical wings served as administrative offices, servants' quarters, barns, warehouses, and so forth. This echoed the arrangement of ancient country estates of the Roman gentry and reflected the ideal Late Republican and Early Imperial social order.

Vasari's brief biography of Palladio is little more than a brisk inventory of building projects and the names of those who commissioned them. But he notes that: "with all this ability, he possesses an affable and courteous disposition which renders him a favourite with all."[30] He seems to have gotten on well with both the highborn and powerful for whom he worked and with the humblest of those who worked for him. Though he was always in demand, it does not seem he made a great deal of money. All his life, he lived in leased premises. He never owned property.

"Poor old Andrea," said his friend, the painter Magagno, "Whatever he earned, he spent it all."[31]

Although the great wars that had cut through northern Italy at the end of the preceding century had come to an end, Palladio did not live in a world of settled civic life. Many of his clients were locked in endless internecine feuds. The Thiene, Loschi, Almerico, Capra, Godi, Piovene, Valmarana, da Roma, and Pagliarino families, all clients of Palladio's, were variously involved in killing each other either personally or hiring gangs of assassins to do so. As an alternative, denunciations to the Inquisition sometimes sufficed. Palladio's first patron, Giangiorgio Trissino, was pulled out of bed and thrown onto the street by his son, Giulio, on Christmas Eve of 1547. Giulio then seized the villa on which Palladio had first collaborated ten years earlier.

And such mayhem was not restricted to aristocrats; in 1569, Palladio's eldest son, Lionida, while drinking, took offense at his host's remarks and stabbed him to death. Three years later, he himself was murdered. There are almost no documents conveying any sense of Palladio's inner life, but in a note to an employer asking forgiveness for delaying some work, he said that his son's death had caused him to be "hindered and troubled both in soul and body."[32] Orazio, one of Palladio's most hardworking sons, was investigated by the office of the Inquisition two years after Lionida's crime and died suddenly shortly before his violent brother's murder.

In the last ten years of Palladio's life, there was a shift. He no longer held so precisely to the numerical proportions of his earlier designs. The frontal columns became higher, and, more than ever before, he emphasized the purely decorative impact of such exterior elements. James Ackerman has commented at length on the way Palladio seems to have been drawn to more atmospheric effects and took a greater interest in how light and shadow influenced the perception of his buildings. He was more calculating about how ambient light affected the way the decor of a facade could be made to look deeper, shallower, darker, or lighter. Natural light became an active element in his church interiors as they bathed its surfaces and articulating the interior space with reflected radiance and deep shadow. In both exterior and interiors, light, and the shifts of light throughout the day, made the stone and stucco seem less densely material, less weighty, and somehow more expressive of a luminous translucent beauty.[33]

Palladio undertook the design of his last buildings two years after the terrible plague from 1575–1576 which had killed a third of the Venetian populace. These two buildings, contrasting in method and intent, were the Church of the Most Holy Redeemer (Il Redentore) on the Guidecca in Venice and the Teatro Olimpico in Vicenza.

With Il Redentore, he created a structure of refined verticality which seems to rise almost weightlessly. The clarity of its proportions produces a feeling of motionless simplicity in the body of the church and of airy lightness in the dome. The church as a whole seems part of a world no longer burdened by the plague-borne devastation, terror, and corpse-filled streets which were the impetus for its existence. The pale luminous interior is breathtaking in its stillness, remote from despair and grief. "The light does more than illumine [...]. Its different quality in each of the three major spaces (nave, tribune, choir) underlines their individuality, [... and] the white blaze of the choir against which the columns [...] are silhouetted become immaterial and attracts one as if to a supernal goal."[34] The harsh materiality of the world is here transformed into a refuge and prayer, where pain and panic dissolve in luminous, all-encompassing peace.

Constructed at the same time as this extraordinary church, the Teatro Olimpico in Vicenza was built for the Accademia Olimpica, the renowned center for humanist learning whose members included Palladio and the late Trissini. The Teatro Olimipico is unlike any other structure Palladio designed or anything seen anywhere else. This is the first permanently enclosed theater built in Italy. Before that, all theaters were open-air, and the audience looked from ranked semi-circular seating, down onto a stage which had a proscenium behind. Palladio had studied and written about Roman architecture in detail and was familiar with such theaters. But, for his final building, he made something completely new.

He made a building that is outside in. The exterior of the theater is a non-descript façade of brick and the rusticated columns from an abandoned fortress; it is almost unnoticeable. Inside is another world. A rising crescent of seats are arranged as in a Roman amphitheater; behind and above rises a portico surmounted by statues of men in classical robes. The ceiling is curved and painted like a sky with racing clouds.

The viewers, as if they were outdoors, look down at a great proscenium, a wide, three-storied façade, rising in classical orders and surmounted by statuary depicting the building's donors wearing Roman togas. Through its large central gate, the viewers see the buildings of a great city ranged along a central avenue, diminishing in size as they reach a vanishing point. This permanent set was lit by a novel and intricate arrangement of candles and oil lamps, carefully focused to resemble daylight but shielded to prevent the set from catching fire. It may not have been designed by Palladio who died before the theater was finished.

Throughout his long career, Palladio had provided settings that gave great families a pattern and style for their extravagant passions and cultural ambitions. The exterior of one of Palladio's most renowned villas, the Palazzo Barbaro, had again displayed the balanced symmetrical expanses which he and his patrons esteemed. But here, Giambattista Tiepolo painted its interiors in ravishingly sensuous detail with fanciful murals which cleverly presented the illusions of surrounding parks and doors to them. Thus, when the owners entertained their guests, gave balls and banquets, they wandered, as if in a dream, through spaces where inside and outside, illusion and reality were indistinguishable.

In the Teatro Olimpico, Palladio made this illusion even more complete: the interior was an exterior, a space where the audience could inhabit a new world of memory, a classical past, isolated from all the madness of the chaos outside. It was as if they were evolving a new carapace. Here, in the orderly vistas of a humanist utopia, they could watch plays in which violent passions were manifest, understood, and resolved. In so doing, the audience, who were otherwise caught up in endless chaotic tumult, became part of a larger, much older, and more harmonious order. Here, Palladio, in his very last work, fulfilled this illusion.

Palladio died before the theater was complete, but it was finally finished, though his plans were somewhat altered, by a jealous colleague. Now, the Teatro Olimpico still exists and with it, our completely illusory dream of an order in which the past is transformed, and our desperate passions transcended.

* * *

My neighbor's spine is crumbling, and it has become impossible for her to visit friends or to sit in a chair long enough for them to visit her. Her daughters are attentive and call daily; she enjoys their conversation and they hers. She has become accustomed to the absence of her many friends, but, when she hears of their deaths, she does not grieve. Rather, as she says, there is a feeling of completion. Now she can see the whole shape of their lives.

IV

Domains of Loss

When the world ends, and the fires blaze unobstructedly
through everything, and all falls to ruin, we just follow
circumstance.

— Dogen, "Thirty-seven Pieces of Dharma"[1]

As we age, we feel our bodies becoming more fragile, less capable; we sense that our minds move more haphazardly. We are less at home in the world. We begin to experience our aging bodies and fading perceptual faculties as restricting and confining us. This is a "galling limitation,"[2] as the *Yijing* puts it, and here the hexagram supplies the larger context: "Limitation means stopping."[3] Thus in reaction to new constraints, our minds often take flight in journeys elsewhere. Now we are entering the time we all have feared, have hoped, and pretended could not happen. A time we cannot exactly imagine. Even as we saw parents, relatives, and friends decline, become incapable, incontinent, their minds adrift further and further from familiar shores, we somehow believed that if we did not pay close attention, this simply would not happen to us.

But we all know that as we age, unforeseeable things will happen to us, will be done to us. No plans or calculations will enable us to escape. We know we will not have the capacities to resist. Atul Gawande, a distinguished surgeon and commentator on the care of the aged, describes the likely situation in which we who live in the Western post-industrial world will find ourselves:

> The waning days of our lives are given over to treatments that addle our brains and sap our bodies of a sliver's chance of benefit. They are spent in institutions — nursing homes and intensive care units — where regimented, anonymous routines cut us off from all the things that matter to us in life. Our reluctance to honestly examine the experience of aging and dying has increased the harm we inflict on people and denied them the comforts they most need. Lacking a coherent view of how people might live successfully all the way to their very end, we have allowed our fates to be controlled by the imperatives of medicine, technology, and strangers.[4]

And even if we are fortunate enough to be able to afford a relatively agreeable old age home or assisted living facility, once we have been moved into such a place, we will no longer be considered full members of the living world. We will find ourselves in a kind of bardo where friends, family, doctors, and caregivers no longer think of us as exactly alive. We will wield no influence in the outer world and will have few ways of controlling the specifics of our daily lives such as diet, whom we live with, times we wake, sleep, bathe, read, what we watch on TV, and so on. Such choices will no longer be left to us.

* * *

ROBERT WALSER (1878–1956)

The Swiss-German writer Robert Walser wrote art reviews, short stories, plays, novels, and feuilletons. He rarely made enough money to survive and was often evicted from his small, rented rooms. Sometimes, he'd move in with relatives, most happily with his brother Karl, a successful painter and set designer, in

Berlin. On other occasions, he took up strangely anonymous forms of employment. His superb handwriting allowed him to work as a clerk and copyist; his peculiarly stubborn servility led to work as a butler. Always, something went wrong. He got in arguments with his employers. His clumsy, earnest flirtations gave offense. His uncertain stance and manner were always slightly disturbing.

However, this oblique estrangement, always present in his work, somehow struck a chord with other writers of his time. "Scarcely has he taken up his pen than he is overwhelmed by a mood of desperation. Everything seems on be on the verge of disaster; a torrent of words pours from him in which the only point of every sentence is to make the reader forget the previous one."[5] When Walter Benjamin wrote these words, this atmosphere resonated with the social and financial catastrophes of 1929, and such uncertainty may play a part in Walser's reception now. In the same year, Walser's hesitant but oddly penetrating essay about Cézanne was published. He talks about the painter's relationship to the fruits and flowers in his still lives and even more, he speculates on Cézanne's wife. He speaks of each picture as if it were a person, and he concludes:

> All the things Cézanne grasped became intermarried, and if we find it proper to speak of his musicality, it was from the plenitude of this observation that it sprang, and from his asking each object if it might agree to give him a revelation of its essence, and most preeminently from his placing in the same "temple" things both large and small.

> The things he contemplated become eloquent, and the things to which he gave shape looked back at him as if they had been pleased, and that is how they look at us still.[6]

In 1931 Walser was 51, and the rigors of marginal existence had taken their toll. Even his sister could no longer look after him. She committed him to a mental institution at Waldau in his native Switzerland. "The patient confessed hearing voices," it said on his admission form. There, he went on long walks and continued writing and publishing.

When he was moved to a sanitorium in the Appenzell region, he said he had stopped writing. He told his devoted friend Carl Seelig: "I am not here to write, but to be mad."[7] But actually, he found a new way of exploring his inner life by doing both. Secretly, as if he were a spy sending messages to an alien power, he wrote tiny essays and stories in minute, self-invented coded script on the back of random bits of paper which he carefully hid away.

The following was written in Walser's minute, crabbed cypher on the back of the business card of a fabric store (*Import Englisher Stoffe / HANS MARTY/ Burgdorf/ telefon 89*). It concludes a piece he titled "New Year's Page":

> I can't seem to resist the thought that at present we frequently have opportunity to read about crises and the like. Apparently it is practically a matter of *bon ton* nowadays to find oneself in a crisis of some sort.

> How lovely the Christmas season was a few years ago. I walked silently through the streets, the ringing bells and silvery snowflakes. The casual manner in which I loved my beloved, who was forever distinguishing herself by her utter absence, resembled a soft-swelling, enchanting sofa. A much-loved authoress was at just this time delighting her followers with a charming new book. New Year's? Don't the words almost smell a bit of wistfulness? When a year stops, another instantly commences, as if one were turning a page. The story keeps on going, and the beauty of a context is revealed.[8]

What was he doing? In this writing, Walser seems to have found a way of simultaneously unifying, concealing, exploring, and preserving the voices that surfaced in his awareness. As he wrote, he drew on linkages formed with the inherited store of words, syntactic structures, images, and tropes. Here he found shape and direction for the chaotic flow of thoughts, memories, and wishes: a way in which disparate voices might reveal place, coherence, and allure. This journey in words led him further and further away from the ordinary world but allowed him to remain, even now, in a realm where we can meet him still.

* * *

According to the us Centers for Disease Control:

> People with dementia often have symptoms like trouble remembering, thinking, or making everyday decisions. These symptoms tend to get worse over time. [...] Symptoms include problems with short-term memory, paying bills, preparing meals, remembering appointments, or getting lost in familiar areas.[9]

According to the Alzheimer's Association, "the percentage of people with Alzheimer's dementia increases dramatically with age: 3 percent of people age 65–74, 17 percent of people age 75–84, and 32 percent of people age 85 or older have Alzheimer's dementia."[10]

Most of us now are far more afraid of becoming demented and institutionalized than we are of dying. We are afraid of being incapable of taking care of ourselves, of becoming "management issues," objects of pained revulsion, incomprehension, or strained forbearance. And no one knows what those of us who require such care will experience inwardly. No one knows the struggles, obstacles, the discoveries we may encounter within. At that point, we are living elsewhere. And who can know this journey entrapped in the body, unable to walk, thirsty, breathless: the anxious advances through the claustrophobic shadows of Piranesi-like prisons, the sudden bursts of light, the feeling of being on the verge of a vast and unimpeded expanse, the fear?[11]

The borders of our existence contract; the familiar becomes remote. The body and the world we know are only partly ours. Our feelings thoughts, memories, all that now concern us are no longer so strongly tied to exterior frames of reference.

Our body and its continuity have become the domain of others. Constrained within our physical collapse, our untethered minds drift in exile. Our mind stream is tantalizing, suggestive, revealing, deeply meaningful, and sometimes utterly terrifying as when the prisoners are shown devices to be used in torturing them. We wander anxiously or with hopeful curiosity in this inner world, looking for doors, gates, stairs, for ways out.

We are imprisoned in our wasting bodies and surrender, bit by bit, our abilities to function, to communicate, to meet the expectations of daily life. Those who attend us as our end nears can only judge our inner voyages by inference. Those who watch see little but deterioration, frustration, confusion; they cannot see if there may be pathways that open deep within, journeys taken between sleep and death.

*　*　*

LOUIS-AUGUSTE BLANQUI (1805–1881)

Louis-Auguste Blanqui was a life-long radical agitator, and, for more than forty years, he advocated the violent overthrow of whatever government ruled France. He was the most feared man in the country, convicted many times for sedition, treason, revolution, and so forth. Once he was sentenced to death, another time to exile. Every government imprisoned him. He spent most of his life in locked cells. His longest term of incarceration took place in the Fort du Taurreau, a fortified island in the North Sea, half a mile off the French coast. The fortress was made of granite, and Blanqui was its only prisoner. His health was already broken, but he was confined to a small room with damp stone walls, small windows placed so that he could not see the world. Above him loomed a dark domed ceiling. He was in constant pain. Occasionally, he was allowed to exercise in a walled courtyard, but his guards had orders to shoot him if he came near any portal through which he could see outside. He was, after all, the most effective and most dangerous political operative in France. He had no reason to believe he would ever leave this prison alive. He was a living dead man.

When he was 65, at the outset of his life sentence in Fort de Taurreau, Blanqui began writing *Eternity by the Stars*. His claustrophobia then was total, both in space and time. His circumstances were unalterable. In this extraordinary book, he wrote of what he saw from this terminal vantage point. In the dimensions of mind alone, he was drawn into boundless space and the infinity of galaxies of stars. Time likewise expanded before him without measurement or limit. Eternity was something he knew and could see. He was allowed to write, and he transcribed the vision of the continuing rhythms of material existence that appeared to him in the light of infinite time.

> Any celestial body, whatever it is, exists in infinite numbers in time and space, not only under one of its aspects, but such that it appears at every second of its life span, from its birth till its death. Every being great or small, live or inert, that is spread over its surface, shares the privilege of this immortality.

> The earth is one of these celestial bodies. Therefore every human being is eternal at every second of its existence. That which I am writing at this moment, in a dungeon of the Fort du Taureau, I have written and shall write again forever, on a table, with a quill, under clothes and in almost entirely similar circumstances. And so it is for all of us.

> All of these earths stumble, one after the other, into the rejuvenating flames, so to be born again and to stumble again, in the monotonous flow of an hourglass eternally turning itself over and emptying itself. What we have is ever-old newness & ever-new oldness.[12]

> At the present hour, the entire life of our planet, from its birth to its death, unfolds, day by day, on myriads of twinglobes, with all the same crimes and misery. [...] Always

and everywhere [...], the same drama, the same set, on the
same narrow stage, a noisy humanity, infatuated by its own
greatness, thinking itself to be the universe and inhabiting its
prison like an immensity, only to drown soon along with the
globe that has borne the burden of its pride with the deepest
scorn. The same monotony, the same immobility in the foreign stars. The universe repeats itself endlessly [...]. Unfazed,
eternity plays the same performance in the infinite.[13]

In his extremity, Blanqui saw an infinity of intersecting parallel universes, each almost identical, each moving through time
simultaneously with all the others so that the totality of possibilities and outcomes of every conceivable kind is all happening at
once without conflict or interruption. It is a universe where no
ambition, desire, goal, whether base or noble, can be blocked.
No being can be erased or forever hidden. It is a universe in
which each passing moment is, at the same time, eternal and
inseparably filled with every other conceivable moment.

He lived with nothing but this vision for eight years and it
never left him, even when, in a strange, almost ridiculous turn
of events, the people of Bordeaux elected him to the chamber
of deputies as their representative. Many thought the vote had
been rigged, but since he was then an elected official, the government was required to release him. He had little strength but
immediately resumed political agitating. In December of 1880,
after giving a fiery speech again urging revolution, he collapsed
from a stroke and soon after died. In this world, certainly and
no doubt in many others, his life ended, and its causes failed.
But perhaps elsewhere, if his prison visions truly penetrated the
veils of ignorance and delusion that blind us here, things are
very different and more in line with what Blanqui sought. We do
not know which version a reader may now inhabit.

* * *

When old, all the arrangements are less stable. The realities and
capacities of now may, at any time, bend and buckle.

Nonetheless, it becomes clear that while in earlier parts of life, one might be forging some kind of personal identity, now, in old age, individuality dissolves. One may look back but cannot go there. No one can imagine getting old, at all. We simply can't. Transient global amnesia, something that rarely affects the young, is an experience of complete disappearance. And this because old age is the dissolution of identity. It just is.

But life, living, shimmering in the unceasing movements of shift, of falling, of electricity and brain waves, we, even as we dissolve, still can see it, smell and taste and touch it, hear it. Thus, we cannot help now but be and sing the world so revealed in its (our) passing splendor, love, and tenderness: sunset, golden pink, magenta, black, screaming, fills the blank sky above a cold, withdrawing tide.

Inner worlds emerge, seductive in pale skies above the hard shiny tree leaves; a violin's attack uncoils; we see the swooping black wing of one crow then another and another; feel sadness sliding in behind a sudden feeling of love; recall the tart–sweet taste of blackberry as its taut skin give way, then seeds crunched, a little bitter; remember the rhythmic extension of a marble colonnade, and above it, sculpted saints, gold domes shimmering, then the faint perfume in an empty corridor, the dream of a friend visiting unexpectedly that foretells… what? What is remembered here? What is not remembered?

Shapes and rhythms unfold, wave upon wave moving forward like terraces, rising in white foam at the front, cresting, breaking, and on. The shimmer of transient meanings within the interplay of colors, sounds, tastes, smells open, expand, break apart. The breaking waves, the salt in air, the filtered brightness of the sun.

And, as one surrenders to each moment, even as one washes a fork, the idea of the observer begins to melt. The observer, the knower, the experiencer moves in and out, becomes, for a moment then another, unnecessary. The focus is melting as phenomena ceaselessly, generously unfold.

We are being melted into air and density and sound and bitterness and awareness altogether which has no future, past, or purpose. Held here by mountains; a night bright with the fires that light the dark. And freeze, captured by stars.

Now I am catching flickers of experience in this net of words (its history of linked distinctions) because I am thinking of you, a you I perhaps have yet to meet. Words serve to bind momentary patterns in a larger human pattern, its history, its social orbits with their exchanges and its weaving. There may be companionship, there where you are sitting, and perhaps a kind of pleasure.

The extravagance of our heart–mind untethered, its uncontrolled outpourings are overwhelming, delirious, frightening. Abandoned from without, turned inward, we wander in a jungle, overwhelmed by smells of perfume and rot, and bird song and monkey screams, and insects, reptiles, predatory cats, deadly disease. It is easy to lose our way, to follow one trail then another, walk beside one stream, hoping to reach the sea. 1500 years ago, in central China, Li Bo sang: "If you're not drunk yet, how will you ever find your way home?"[14]

* * *

NICOLAS CALAS (1907–1988)

When I first met Nico, he was in his waning prime. Cavafy and others he had known as a young man in Greece were long gone. His Paris friends, André Breton, Antonin Artaud, Paul Éluard, René Crevel, Salvador Dalì, Louis Aragon, Marcel Duchamp, Max Ernst, among others, were dead. And the circles in which he enjoyed more recent celebrity, including Arshile Gorky, Peggy Guggenheim, Jasper Johns, and Robert Rauschenberg, had also died or left him behind. His poetry was still admired in Greece, but the *Village Voice, Art Forum,* and other magazines had less and less use for his essays on contemporary art. With the disappearance of the contexts in which he'd flourished, his ways of thinking seemed somehow less penetrating. But with his great height, strong nose, and glittering black eyes, he looked like an aging eagle stranded on a mountaintop. His orator's voice, with the plosive accents of his native Greek, was still commanding, and his erudite wit was still part of an imposing display.

At a dinner in the early seventies given by fellow art critic and sometimes rival, Lawrence Alloway, the conversation turned to the late paintings of Giorgio de Chirico. Alloway maintained they were utterly trivial.

"Trivial like Fragonard?" asked Nico.

"Yes."

"Well to paint trivially in a manner such as that, in an age such as this is an act of profound stoicism." And he surveyed the table with a gleam of self-satisfaction at his turn of phrase.

At tea one afternoon, he proclaimed: "The accomplishment of Freud is that he renewed the compact of Abraham."

And later: "I like John Ashbery. He has turned Henry James into prose."

One afternoon when he was ill, he took special pains to tell me the story of an Austrian Prime Minister who had been famous for his cleverness, but who, in a speech, had made some kind of gaffe. "Ah, intelligence ages," twitted some young wag. "Stupidity never," the Prime Minister spat back.

Circumstances took me away from New York for almost eight years, and when I returned, I resumed visiting Nico regularly. He had abandoned all interest in current or even recent art and was devoting himself to a commentary that would solve all the "riddles" in the painting of Hieronymus Bosch. "I have begun a new phase and discovered something revolutionary," he asserted. Like his other remaining friends and also his wife, I found his claims about the painter both perverse and wantonly obscure.

He contended, without the support of historical evidence, that Bosch's phantasmagoria embodied controversies debated by Saint Augustine, Porphyry, Origen, and other great figures of the early Eastern Church. This was, in Nico's view, the only way to explain the complexities of the paintings. On each visit, he would repeat the same argument: a section of the Odyssey refers to a cave in which naiads weave cloth on looms made from or resembling jars. Porphyry had commented on this passage and had been refuted by Augustine. The eggs or testicular shapes in the paintings, according to Nico, referred to the jars in Homer and were thus clear references to this theological disagreement. Nico would point a long finger at various images in a book of reproductions and proclaim: "See! See! It's right there."

I told him I simply didn't see it and tried to suggest other ways of exploring his otherwise opaque assertion. He didn't care. He felt the truth of his argument was self-evident, and somehow, the Bollingen Foundation saw fit to give him a lavish grant to pursue these inquiries. "My wife believes my research on Bosch has ruined my career. She even says it has ruined her life," he would say with a mixture of defiance and complacency.

Nico and I repeated this conversation many times. Eventually I came to feel that his absorption in Bosch was his way of circumventing a life-long commitment to his Marx-tinged Surrealism and of coming to terms with the last things. I also realized that his wife's bitterness came not just from her hard-headed opposition to looniness in general, but because she saw that this project was Nico's vehicle for withdrawing from life altogether.

Nico's three invariant questions in the time after the Bosch business subsided were: "Have you seen X?" (An art dealer I hadn't seen in ten years); "Have you seen Y?" (An artist and his wife whom I saw often); and "Have you been to any galleries? (Which I rarely had).

"How are you?" I asked. Though it was late afternoon, Nico was seated on his unmade bed, unshaven and not yet fully dressed.

"Nonexistent."

"And how is that?"

"I have reached another stage."

"Ah."

"You agree?"

"Yes."

We sat together and drank tea from not very clean cups. Nico was silent, and somehow, I felt as if the two of us were at the seaside, looking out on a gray exhausted sea whose feeble oily waves still managed to lap the shore.

Nico's wife told me that every morning he came into her room before she woke and in a loud voice announced either: "Today I am going to die." Or "Today we are going back to Greece."

The business of going to Greece was a physical impossibility that had nonetheless obsessed him for some months. It dwelled deep in his mind. He was anxious to visit a commune of young Russian poets whom he was sure were living there. They were wholly imaginary, and the fact was that he had no living relatives or friends in Greece, no home or place to stay and no one to help him except his wife who was herself unwell and utterly unwilling. But Nico had become so persistent that finally she considered putting him on an airplane by himself. She knew that should she do so, it was unlikely she would ever see him again, but felt since he was so desperate to go, perhaps he should. She insisted I speak to him about this.

"If you go, don't you think you might die there?" I asked.

"No. That's not the point."

"Then it's some kind of renewal?"

"Yes."

A week later: "I'm completely bored," said Nico.

"I've spent a lot of time becoming accustomed to that," I reply.

"Is that a Buddhist thing?"

"Yes."

"We have more in common than I thought."

Nico was now sitting in a wheelchair, looking disordered and out of it. His wife was also in the room, ignoring him as she drank tea fortified with vodka.

Nico said in a combative tone, "I feel as if I died already."

"Me too," I said, a bit too casually.

Nico gave a cracked smile. "Why then, we're having a post-mortem conversation."

I then told a long story from Saint-Simon's memoires about the Prince de Condé who had a scientific but fundamentally weird turn of mind. This prince, by weighing his excrement and urine and comparing that to the weight of his food and drink, concluded, since there was no difference between the two, that he was dead. Quite logically he saw no further reason to continue eating and began slowly to starve to death. His doctor was distressed but solved the problem by hiring a troupe of actors who would sit down to dinner with the Prince and explain that, while they too were dead, they ate. The Prince accepted their contention, and the ensuing table talk about their shared post-mortem condition was a cause of great hilarity to the ingenious doctor.

Nico and his wife both laughed, and this was one of the few occasions when they seemed to share any pleasure.

Some weeks later: "What are you thinking about these days?" I asked Nico.

"I am in the process of losing all interest in things."

"Does that feel dull or bright?"

He waved his large, gnarled hand in a gesture of vague dismissal. A little later he said,

"I am dying."

"I know." We looked at each other for a while until he turned away.

"Are you apprehensive?" I asked.

"Somewhat." Another long pause. "You see, I've made a mistake."

"What's that?"

"What I told you before."

"The losing interest?"

"Yes."

When Nico's wife fell and had to be hospitalized, he became deranged and violent and had to be institutionalized. The place was modern, clean, and well run, but as I walked down the waxed gray linoleum of the halls, it seemed all the residents had sunk into a distressing similarity. Pasty, slack-jawed, in faded bathrobes, those not actively dying sat parked in wheelchairs and stared intently into air. Two asked for candy, another for his wallet. Whoever these people had been, all that remained were the flotsam of character, tossed up randomly on this scrubbed anonymous shore, relics of some unimaginable catastrophe.

Nico was lying in a dark room next to a comatose man. A doctor in the shadows was talking softly to him, explaining where he was and why he was there. Nico said nothing but wept silently. I interrupted and told him Nico understood, then, in an effort to get the doctor to think of him with some measure of individuality, explained that his patient was an eminent man.

The doctor nodded and left. Nico finally fell asleep.

The day before he died, Nico was mumbling urgently in broken Greek. I said, "Nico, you know I can't speak Greek." He sat up and looked blankly at me. If he had been lying down, I would have thought he was dead. His skin was a waxy gray-green; his nose had receded at the bridge and looked even more beak-like; his cheeks had sunk and his dark eyes were lusterless and opaque. But I had brought him a box of cookies. He grabbed them and shoved them into his mouth two at a time. Crumbs flew everywhere.

He subsided into a stupor, and suddenly lay back down. Now a fluttering liquid rasp was the only, and short-lived, evidence he was still alive.

* * *

It is now quite common to think of those whom we used to call senile and now call demented as so estranged that they are no longer part of our shared human journey. They have become deviant. We look on them with ill-concealed horror. We struggle to act as if they were still human but speak to them as pets or children. We shut out any sense that we might share their fate, though there is a statistical likelihood that we will do so. And today, so many people live so much longer that dementia for us is more than a possibility. How we might then continue and what our relationship to the world might mean is a pervasive question.

Maurice Merleau-Ponty pointed to the seeds of a fresh, but perhaps more ancient outlook when he said: "The things of the world are not simply neutral objects before our contemplation; each symbolizes or recalls a certain mode of conduct... each speaks to our body and to our life." Things "haunt our dreams," they are "clothed in human characteristics," and "they dwell in us as emblems of behavior we either love or hate."[15]

The anthropologist Eduardo Kohn, took a similar journey in his efforts to comprehend the complex fields of meaning experienced and shared by those who live in the dense chaotic life of the Amazon jungle. Kohn spent four years in Ecuador's upper Amazon living with and learning from the Runa people. His book *How Forests Think* explores the profoundly intersubjective and interspecies ecology of forest flora, fauna, and forest dwellers. The Runa survive amid violent storms and floods; endure the depredations of bandits, government officials, and rubber tappers; and survive by hunting birds, tapirs, fish, finding root vegetables. To endure, they rely not so much on inferences derived from exterior scientific uniformities as on intuition, ancestral lore, visions; a kind of inwardness that gives them flexible and constant links into the living world. Here, the "spirit realm that emerges from the life of the forest, as a product of a whole host of relations that cross species lines and temporal epochs, is, then, a zone of continuity and possibility."[16] Survival

> depends on the many kinds of dead and the many kinds of deaths that this spirit realm holds in its configuration and that make a living future possible. Who one might be is intimately related to all those who one is not; we are forever giving ourselves over and indebted to those many others who make us who "we" are.[17]

At one point, Kohn speaks of a dream he'd had and discussed with some of his Indigenous informants.

> I've come to wonder how much of my dream was ever really my own; for a moment, perhaps, my thinking became one with how the forest thinks. Perhaps [...] there is indeed something about such dreams which "think in men unbeknownst to them." Dreaming may be, then, a sort of thought run wild — a human form of thinking that goes well beyond the human [...]. Dreaming is a sort of *"pensée sauvage"*: a

human form of thinking unfettered from its own intentions and therefore susceptible to the play of forms in which it has become immersed — which, in my case […] is one that gets caught up and amplified in the multispecies, memory-laden wilderness of an Amazon forest.[18]

What Kohn describes is a specific way our inner life organically interpenetrates and is interpenetrated by our outer environment. This is a kind of experiencing common throughout our history and world. Meaning, in this context, is not based on convention, fixed references, social purpose or intent, but on more extensive, free-flowing associations, and intuitive, multidimensional linkages. Kohn continues:

> This kind of exploratory freedom is I think what Claude Lévi-Strauss was getting at when he wrote of savage thought as "mind in its untamed state as distinct from mind cultivated or domesticated for the purpose of yielding a return." It is also something, I believe, that Sigmund Freud grasped in his recognition of how the unconscious partakes of the kind of self-organizing logic to which Levi-Strauss is alluding. […] Freud's insight, gesturing quite literally to an "ecology of mind," was to develop ways to become aware of these iconic associative chains of thought (and even to find ways to encourage them to proliferate) and then, by observing them, to learn something about the inner forests these thoughts explore as they resonate through the psyche.[19]

It may be worth noting that Lévi-Strauss observed:

> [W]hether one deplores it or rejoices in it, zones are still known in which wild thought, like wild species, is relatively protected. Such is the case of art, to which our civilization gives the status of a national park, with all the advantages and disadvantages attaching to such an artificial formula.[20]

* * *

ALEXANDER DREIER (1949–2019)

Alexander Dreier was very much a product of New England. His father was a career diplomat and his mother a gifted and quirky painter. He was a profoundly ethical and creative man, fortunate that his circumstances allowed, even encouraged him to pursue interests and commitments infrequently followed by others. He was a farmer, therapist, poet, and comedian, dedicated to implementing the spiritual and ecological thinking of Rudolf Steiner. In 1963, he was diagnosed with Lewy Body dementia, a disorder which produces disorientation, hallucinations, and then extreme dementia. Finally, it caused his death.

Dreier did not merely accept his diagnosis; he accepted his disease as a field of exploration. He engaged the chaos of strange phenomena which he then experienced as sequences of adventures, marvels, tests, and revelations. He wrote an account of this journey in poetry and prose, and made it available in his extraordinary book, *The Brain Is a Boundary*. The prose portion of the book begins:

> In the summer of 2014, on an early morning walk near our cabin on an island off the coast of Maine, where I was enjoying a solitary retreat, I came across a group of indigenous looking children dressed in clothes made of leaves. Ignoring my greeting, they followed me right into the house where their apparent ringleader, a three-foot tall man with dreadlocks, who appeared to have a hose coming out of his head, was engaging a group of adults in some kind of ritual. Fascinated as I was by their ceremonies which involved magical screens and spinning trees, I eventually called the local sheriff to have them removed from the property. It was then after 10 pm. They had long overstayed their welcome and refused to respond to my most basic questions:
>
> "Who are you? Why are you here? What are you doing?" The next day, my wife, Olivia and my brother-in-law arrived and

finally convinced me that this strange cast of characters had all been a very long "waking dream."[21]

This was all part of Dreier's clear-eyed and direct exploration of a disorderly world in which waking life and dreams are not segregated but interpenetrate unpredictably and continuously. He did not wish to banish or eliminate these often inconvenient if slightly numinous phenomena. He tried to negotiate a way of living in this unstable world which might without warning veer between the radiant, the seductive, and the darkly ominous. This involved seeing the cosmos as more porous, more pregnant with images and meanings, and it involved regarding himself in a different way.

As to the former, he said:

> In my experience, things that are ordinary often become extraordinary. This then presents me with an invitation to encounter that extraordinariness in whatever way I am able or willing [...]. The medicines I am taking keep this often-surprising imagery at a level where it mostly does not alarm me but rather, in all kinds of interesting ways, leads me to question what I am seeing. I do have difficulty working with the normal dimensions of time.[22]

Dreier's friend, Arthur Zajonc, who also explored a diverging inner life as he worked with his Parkinson's disease, put it this way: "For people like Alexander and me, the solid grounding offered by outer experience may be weakened so that the mind is less tightly tethered to the sense world."[23] Dreier said in a poem that he found that "only the sky is his one true brain."[24] And so, one of his last poems:

The Messenger

Who but the last cloud
Knows what this isthmus is,
Not narrow mined but ground,

Down where arrival is departure,

Where contrails of sweat-soaked
Expectations slip into streaming
Blue lightness? Who do eyes see
Without the cartload of luggage we

Gathered up before words,
When I first noticed you at the
Fiery open threshold, wearing
The dusty old hat of the universe?

You were arresting, radiant palms,
Facing the midheaven, where
The cusp was in big beginning
Of the whole high domicile,

Meridians alive for all to feel.
Yes you, transparent crescent
Of becoming, as the gateway
To the liminal horizon, as
Messenger of the not yet born.[25]

* * *

To aging people, to dying ones, the world is less credible, less
necessary. Those who do not maintain a hold on context are
diagnosed with mental disorders, and certainly they may no
longer be able to care for themselves, but perhaps they are now
searching elsewhere. They are, it may be, drawn into some other
form of being, a symbiont mind. There is no longer defining
anything or guiding anything, winnowing grain from chaff,
or moving toward any future. There is only a feeling of being
moved this way and that and being eased or pained in heat or
cold. And deep within, some different sense of time and linkage
stirs, beginning where nouns and verbs may not be separable.
Or what we call a noun (floor, chair, toilet seat, applesauce) may

in fact (like love, hate, smell, taste, desire) be a verb. And what we call adjectives may then be adverbs (live, dead, true, false). Or further, perhaps what we call language (a mechanism communicating between separate entities but unlike them) may not exist as such, but may be simply the stream of phenomena itself, like a tune, devoid of exterior reference.

Is it then possible that even when we are lost, we can be seeking to be awake? Is it possible that when we are imprisoned in the confines of our own minds, still we are seeking not to dream on but to be free? Paralyzed with fear, lost in the haze and shifting fog, can we be walking on a path we cannot see? If this is so, we cannot prove it. If this is not so, we cannot prove it or disprove it.

* * *

Actually, the conventional boundaries we accept as dividing the inner from the outer in our experience have not always been so definite. Our notion of what kind of experience, or what kind of description of experience is socially acceptable has not always seemed so clear. Sanity and what we now call "insanity" have not always seemed so absolute. Here, for instance, is how Taleisin, the most famous of 6th-century Welsh shape-shifting bards, sang of his waking journey:

> I have been in many shapes
> Before I assumed a constant form:
> I have been a narrow sword,
> A drop in the air,
> A shining bright star,
> A letter among words
> In the book of origins.
> I have been lanternlight
> For a year and a day,
> I have been a bridge
> Spanning three score rivers.
> I have flown as an eagle,

Been a coracle on the sea,
I have been a drop in a shower,
A sword in a hand,
A shield in battle,
A string in a harp.
Nine years in enchantment,
In water, in foam,
I have absorbed fire,
I have been a tree in a covert.
There is nothing of which
I have not been part.
[…]
I have been a snake enchanted on a hill,
I have been a viper in a lake;
I have been a star, crooked at first
The haft of a knife, or a spear in battle.
Clearly shall I prophesy.[26]

* * *

Our forgetting, our delirium, our madness are the flotsam of time past, of passions that left us behind, of knowledge that no longer has an object, of words that suddenly lack definition. We cannot stop moving, and there is no direction. Our time is ending, closing in. A deep fatigue. We may never be able to revisit the Piazza Borghese with its pink, pale blue, and yellow building fragments — a De Chirico background. We were walking but didn't have time to stop, to sit and have a coffee. I thought we'd return. But we didn't, and there must be many wishes to return that float untenanted in the air there.

Ronald Dworkin famously asserted:

By the time the dementia has become advanced, Alzheimer's victims have lost the capacity to think about how to make their lives more successful on the whole. They are ignorant of self — not as an amnesiac is, not simply because they cannot identify their pasts — but, more fundamentally, because they have no sense of a whole life, a past joined to a future, that could be the object of any evaluation or concern as a whole. They cannot have projects or plans of the kind that leading a critical life requires. They therefore have no contemporary opinion about their own critical interests.[27]

This ostensible rationality is strange and perverse. What is "success"? Who can really think of their lives as wholes? We may think about the possible consequences of one or another aspect of one or another set of actions, but we are incapable of thinking about all of them, and it is impossible to imagine that we would think of all of them simultaneously. Dworkin is positing a kind of free rational agent whose authenticity and mental health are defined solely as dependent on accurate and encyclopedic ends–means calculation. There is no one who is like this.

The fact of the matter is that no one knows what is happening in the minds, imaginations, longings, visions of people with Alzheimer's or other forms of dementia. We can, of course, say that their inner lives are increasingly disconnected on the level of short-term memory and speech from a language and frame of reference shared by their contemporaries. This includes losing control of those physical functions that are a foundation of what we consider being adult. Beyond that, what Alzheimer's patients are to themselves, what they think of themselves doing with their lives, their worlds, we simply do not know. No one knows. But to quote from a very different tradition: György Lukács, in his discussion of Thomas Mann's *Death in Venice,* observed, "Everything flows, everything merges into another thing, and the mixture is uncontrolled and impure [...]. To live is to live something through to the end: but life means that nothing is ever fully and completely lived through to the end."[28]

* * *

WILLEM DE KOONING (1904–1997)

In his time, the late 1940s and for three decades on, American painters all thought seriously about their art, drank in prolonged binges, smoked, philandered. They cultivated manliness in hurling themselves past conventional boundaries. This was the received grammar for expressing feeling, understanding, meaning, form. They battled to achieve an art in which the violence of lust or fury or sheer confusion burst in a radiance, a wildness, a confrontational presence in a culture trying to ignore its structural inequities and the damage of two world wars. They set out to make culture democratic, authentic, and brash. No matter their successes and even fame, it was a way of life that took its toll.

After a long career in a turbulent, intensely wrought style of expressionist painting for which he became famous throughout the world, Willem de Kooning went into a long and painful mental decline. His previous paintings were sold for the highest prices which any living artist had ever received. Beginning in the late 1980s, he was diagnosed with Alzheimer's. According to rumor, he barely recognized those close to him or spoke. By using slides of earlier work projected on large canvases and paints mixed and set out before him by assistants, he was able to continue painting for more than ten years.

Some of the more complex pictures were offered for sale during De Kooning's lifetime, and in 1995, the San Francisco Museum of Modern Art and The Walker Art Center presented a large exhibition of this work. The pictures were abstract, almost graphic, and displayed a serenely sophisticated sense of balance and color. It was clear that these new paintings were very different from the artist's previous work. The exhibition was received with great unease, for the artist's medical condition was well known. Though some of the paintings, it was argued, were a reworking of structural elements in earlier works, it also seemed that they were by someone else, or by someone so changed as to be unrecognizable to previous admirers. Some insisted this work was like the late period of other great artists, Claude

Monet, Henri Matisse, and Titian in particular, a radical altera-
tion of working methods and vision. Others found that these
paintings were etiolated and strangely mindless, evidence of a
terrible loss, and represented a cynical, mercenary promotion. It
was, and remains, a disconcerting and uncomfortable situation,
exacerbated, no doubt, by the huge sums of money involved.

The artist was silent, incapable of commenting on his pro-
cesses or intentions. But the fact remains that every day, De
Kooning awoke and painted. One of his earlier works was cho-
sen for him and projected on a blank canvas; paints were set
out. Apparently, he didn't question these choices, but simply set
to work. He continued some kind of journey within his familiar–unfamiliar mind. When his wife died, his daughter asked
the studio assistants to cease using projections. De Kooning, it
was said, was at first puzzled and seemingly lost, but then began
painting concentric circles of different colors. Eyes, hands, and
body, brush, paint, and canvas made available the only world
which he could still explore and perhaps still seduce, love, or
conquer. What it meant to him, what he thought he was doing,
we cannot know. Who was the "inner" here and what was the
"outer"? De Kooning was fortunate that others found this part
of life of value and so supported him.[29]

* * *

Perhaps our inability to create lasting frameworks which can
contain the torrential outpourings of our mind streams (source-
less images, causeless intuitions, unprompted fears, sudden
objectless love, sudden clarity, revulsion, motiveless panic, etc.)
is exactly the point. Perhaps it is when we lose the energy necessary to maintain the social constructs called "functionality" or
"reason" that we may find ourselves adrift in the fevers of this
vast and hidden stream. If so, perhaps we might regard those
we now call demented as simply having followed, accidentally,
even unwillingly, their awareness to another dimension which is
common to us all but which we do not yet have the confidence
to share.

William Kentridge sees this from a different angle: "The world of shadows tells us things about seeing the invisible by the light of the sun. [… T]he source of light […] is both one and separate from one."[30]

V

Domains of Vision

What finally distinguishes old age from all preceding times of life is simply that nothing comes afterward. We will be parted from our body, our world, our language, our past, our frames of reference, our ways of recognizing ourselves, our feelings, our sense of direction. I cannot retain summer skies, my wife's sigh, autumn clouds, my teacher's jokes, my friends' letters, memories of the small black dog who, in the heat of summer, slept on the bathroom's cool tile floor... these things that rise and charm or torment will disappear suddenly, completely, and irreversibly.

What, at that point, we will be or not be, no one knows, and such knowledge may be of no relevance at all. Funerals and rituals may make us and others feel that we remain part of the human realm, that our consciousness is continuing, that the knowable persists. No one can testify to the truth of this, as we, the old, move to the domains of collapse, death, and chaos.

Death is, of course, the final fate of all; the ultimate Other. Indifferent to human wishes, hopes, desires, and projects, it resists integration into society's continuum. As old women and men, our future is no longer part of the urgent social project of continuing. We are headed away from everyone we live with, moving on into something unknowable. We are viewed with subconscious unease. The early Chinese domesticated the dead by transforming deceased ancestors into beneficent deities. But for most of us now, it is most uncertain that dying will serve social goals. At the end of life, we will be unable to feed ourselves; incontinent, we will have relinquished even the most basic social expectations.

Trapped in a falling elevator, imprisoned in a house on fire, we are helpless. We know we're going to die: our mind will be nowhere, our body obliterated, and this will be painful. Beyond that, we have no idea what it means. We cannot really conceive of it, and certainly cannot escape. Our death cannot be navigated. A dying person still does not know what it is to be dead. In one minute, we're one thing and in the next, we're not. We can adopt many ways of thinking about this, but the fact itself is intractable. In old age, we see ourselves, our life, and our world in the light of their flimsiness, their vanity, their unreliability, their final nonexistence.

We are now subject to sequences of transformations that make us unrecognizable, alien even to ourselves. Such incomprehensible changes of form and consciousness are terrifying, and we can see analogies for our own changes in the lives of animals, reptiles, and insects. A caterpillar's change into a butterfly, a metamorphosis we find so intriguing, is, in Dave Goulson's description, a cataclysm of almost unconnected life forms, simultaneous dying and being born continuously, all within a single creature's lifespan.

> Imagine you are a full-grown caterpillar. You digest your final meal of leaves, then spin yourself a silken pad to hold you tight to a stem. You then split out of your old skin, revealing a new, smooth brown skin beneath. You no longer have eyes, or limbs, or any external openings except tiny holes called spiracles to allow you to breathe. You are entirely helpless, and will remain so for weeks, perhaps months [...]. Inside your shiny pupal skin your body dissolves, the cells of your tissues and organs preprogrammed to die and disintegrate, until you are little more than a soup. A few clusters of embryonic cells remain, and these proliferate, growing entirely new organs and structures, building you a brand new body. Once

it is ready, and the time is right, you split open your pupal skin and underneath have grown another one, this time complete with large eyes, a long, coiled proboscis for drinking and beautiful wings covered in iridescent scales that you must inflate by pumping blood into their veins before they harden.[1]

What mind or consciousness, we cannot help but wonder, can retain coherence or continuity through such radical alterations of body? How can there be identity? There is no way to escape the heart-sick terror that such images and thoughts elicit. We can only imagine excruciating bodily pain and mental anguish, as we are consumed in some process so all-encompassing and so terminal. It is paralyzing. At the end, we see that the whole of our life, of all our existence, of all history, of all we have strived for and struggled to accomplish, of all wisdom, courage, or beauty, of all this without exception, is utterly momentary. And nothing will save or redeem us.

We cannot think about this. We can pretend to put it aside, to look away. Beginning and ending are irrelevant. We are carried by an unstoppable force, a rage of continuing, a power that pulls us on and on, inescapable. It is the sheer intensity of experience, of nature. I was visiting a friend in the hospital; her body was giving out, and she could no longer stand or walk. She would die ten days later. "You know what I feel?" she asked. I shook my head. "Vigor."

Continuing, this abidingly visceral force ongoing, does not let us go. It is clearest now in our old age. For no reason, with no logic or reasonable hope, the sheer magnetism of going on moves us and soon will unravel us. At the most subliminal level, like a river hidden deep under a mountain range, yearning, longing, desiring, fearing, hating, continuing, all unraveling; no one thing remaining, but continuing in a flow uninterrupted from each moment to the next. There is no purpose. It is desire or passion or lust or hunger or flight from destruction or appetite or curiosity without any final object. It is the brightness, the desire of desire and love of love. With every atom, it is luminous instinctual continuing, continuing feeling, continuing being and living. It is not good or bad, and it is not involved with pleasure and pain. It is the totality of continuing, tearing through, burning through, falling through the surface of living, and we are swept on as if implacable hatred, utter indifference, and true love all together now took us as their own. And transforming us, body and soul, beyond any limit, beyond anything we will ever recognize or know.

* * *

JOSEPH MALLORD WILLIAM TURNER (1775–1851)

Joseph Mallord William Turner, known in his lifetime as William, was an artistic prodigy born to a London barber and wig-maker. His mother was a butcher's daughter, soon committed to a mental hospital. Turner was a very small, very gifted man, and from his late teens pugnaciously determined to make his living as a painter. Though he maintained many friendships with colleagues and patrons and many intimate relationships with women, these were all subordinate to painting, to maintaining his position in the Royal Academy and to raising the sales price of his work. He was aloof, self-absorbed, proud of maintaining the virtues of a hard-working merchant, and not interested in making his way upward in the English class system. He was, however, educated, knowledgeable about many kinds of culture, and often traveled in Europe. His frequent explorations in Britain brought him in contact not just with the natural landscapes there, but with the blazing fires of industry which he found deeply invigorating. He had no doubts about his abilities and the place he deserved in society and the world of art. He was a man with the passions of his age. He was not shy.

In a famous story, in the Royal Academy Exhibit of 1832, Turner found that his painting, *Helvoetsluys,* a pale seascape he was presenting that year, had been hung next to the more dramatic *Opening of the Waterloo Bridge* by his rival John Constable. It was the custom of the time that on the day before the exhibition opened, the public was invited to watch the artists put the finishing touches on their work. Constable was there when Turner arrived and looked at the two pictures. Realizing that in comparison, his own work lacked drama, he opened his paint box, put some crimson paint on his finger and in the lower center of his canvas, Turner dabbed the form of a red buoy bobbing in the waves. The picture was suddenly transformed from something placid into something intensely dramatic. Turner left immediately. Constable was shocked. "He has been here," he exclaimed, "and he has fired a gun."[2]

Despite his previous successes, in the 1840s many former admirers attacked the direction Turner's art had begun to take. It may seem now that an element of visual abstraction had always been present in his work, but his contemporaries did not see this. Particularly in his last decade of life, his brushwork became more vehement and his colors more intense. Light no longer served just to illuminate land and seascapes, but had become a kind of primordial force, inseparable from the shifting intensity of nature herself.

And critics were increasingly derogatory. According to the watercolorist William Leitch, "Turner used to paint very beautifully 25–30 years before, but his mental state had deteriorated to such an extent that he had become childish. [... E]ven his best friends were not taking his new paintings seriously." William Beckford, builder of Fonthill Abbey and author of *Vathek*, said, "He paints now as if his brains and imagination were mixed up on his palette with soapsuds and lather." More perceptively, he added, "One must be born again to understand his pictures." It was reported in the newspapers that Turner had lost his reason. Cartoons showed him painting, attacking a canvas with a big mop of yellow paint.[3]

Turner's painting *Snow Storm: Steam Boat off a Harbour's Mouth* was exhibited in 1842 and was the occasion for Beckford's "soapsuds and lather" remark. Gleaming slashes of wind-born snow swirl and fill the air, a bank of bright magnesium-white flares blaze above and behind the heaving ship; its dark shadows reach out across waves and troughs. Amid this violent convulsion of light, sea, and wind, the ship itself (as are often in Turner's work, human beings and the things they make) is small and dark, tossed, and utterly at the mercy of forces it had once seemed to master. "I did not paint it to be understood, but I wished to show what such a scene was like; I got the sailors to lash me to the mast to observe it; I was lashed for four hours, and I did not expect to escape, but I felt bound to record it if I did."[4]

Whether the story is true or not is less important than the statement that Turner did not wish this, and no doubt all his work at the time, to be "understood" but to "show what such a scene was like." He was aiming for a connection and engagement with the viewer far deeper and more direct than mere "understanding." He set out to demonstrate the blazing powers of creation and destruction as they pulled together and tore apart the world. He wished to free what he saw from the conventions of the merely pictorial. And he placed man-made objects, ships, bridges, buildings, burning with subversive and uncontrollable energy at the nexus of nature's roiling display. These cataclysmic fires, whether of human origin or natural, seem to burn through surface of the world and the canvas, revealing the elements swirling in primordial chaos. We, the viewer, stand dazzled at the crossroads of creation and destruction.

Turner's work had many defenders, George Jones and Lady Trevelyan among them. She wrote, "in his boundless prodigality of thought, [...] Turner differs from other painters, and [...] the more Turneresque he was the more full of meaning every bit of his work became."[5] John Ruskin, who was Turner's most distinguished and articulate advocate, said in his book *Modern Painters:* the *Snow Storm* painting was "one of the very grandest statements of sea-motion, mist, and light, that has ever been put on canvas."[6] But four years later Ruskin joined those who disparaged Turner's new work. In 1846, he wrote that Turner's painting, *The Angel Standing in the Sun* was "indicative of mental disease."[7] Turner was deeply wounded. "I never forgave him, to his death."[8]

Turner exhibited this painting five years before he died. It is a great blazing whirlpool of orange–white light; at its center a winged angel cries out, brandishing a sword in one hand and making a gesture of warning with the other. In the lower left, a shadowy skeleton, several half-naked people, and a larger demonic creature shrink away into the shades from which flocks of dark birds rise. To the lower right, we see the blurred form of one man encouraging another who sits slumped to rise and make his way up toward welcoming women in white. The sky above them is clearing, and there, many pale birds circle. Two texts were appended to the picture: one, a passage from Revelations 19:17: "And I saw an angel standing in the sun; and he cried with a loud voice, saying to all the fowls that fly in the midst of heaven, Come and gather yourselves together unto the supper of the great God"; the other is a couplet from Samuel Rogers: "The morning march that flashes to the sun? The feast of vultures when the day is done."[9] Perhaps Ruskin was disturbed by the painting's vehement obscurity.

Lady Trevelyan had a different view: "You never get to the end of a picture of his: the more you look at it, the more you find out. [...] Turner's things are really there, and once you have seen them there they are for ever, and you know that he meant them, and meant a thousand things more that you have only to watch for and find out."[10] She ignored the medical critiques that preoccupied Turner's detractors.

But curiosity about physical decline was very much part of contemporary discourse. Turner's one-time physician, Sir Anthony Carlisle, wrote the first book on gerontology in 1835. He had stated, "The age of Sixty may, in general, be fixed upon as the commencement of Senility."[11] And indeed Turner frequently consulted doctors about his many illnesses. He had been stricken with influenza, digestive complaints, fevers, and, for five years, he had to take to bed with some unspecified illnesses. Twice, he broke his kneecap. He contracted cholera twice, the second time in the year before he died. He had a gum infection which required the removal of all his teeth. Turner's illnesses and the kinds of remedies he used to try and cure or at least ameliorate them are a matter of record and well known. He had cataracts, perhaps from staring directly into the sun to understand more fully the colors of its rays. Even so, it is remarkable the extent to which Turner's detractors considered the changes in his work to be of physiological origin and the result of senescence.

Somehow, and though he had many strong admirers, it didn't occur to the critics that Turner was, with ever greater concentration, probing dimensions of reality he had only hinted at when his earlier work had the kind of polish which had made him famous. Seeing an old man, they did not recognize the artist who, even as he was dying, was pursuing something further. "I always dreaded it with horror," Turner said of the ravages of old age.[12] But he pressed on, with resolution, even brio, painting canvases with ever more luminous visions of nature's centipedal violence and the untamable fires always about to consume everything.

To continue working, he hired an assistant and a coachman. He drank quantities of rum and milk because he had no teeth; he drank sherry to lessen his pain. He even had moments of amusement. One evening as he left the Athenaeum with a colleague after an evening of drinking to excess, the friend said that he had double vision and saw two cabs. "That's all right, old fellow," said Turner, "Do as I do. Get into the first one."[13]

When he died, he was, they said, staring at the sun. In an extraordinarily beautiful and precise paragraph, Sam Smiles points to what Turner struggled and sweated to give us, particularly in the last fifteen years of his life.

The world Turner shows is above all dynamic not simply in the obvious sense of picturing storm, fire, and flood as they transform the natural environment, nor in recording the simple fact of movement [...] but in presenting the world as mutable, ever-changing, where solid forms become tremulous in light, water turns into vapour, diurnal and seasonal rhythms of light transmogrify the landscape they illuminate. This ever-shifting world is the stage where humankind plays out its fragile destiny.[14]

* * *

A sunny Saturday afternoon, my wife came home from the beauty parlor. Afterward, as I later recalled, I took her to the hospital (the town's older one) where she needed some kind of tests. The next thing I remember began when I spoke to the nurse in the room she was to occupy, she handed me a gown. "So, my wife's not staying?" "No." "So I'm supposed to stay?" "Right." "Why?" "Because you don't know," she smiled. There was, it tuns out a six-hour gap between these two moments: my wife's return and being handed the gown. The drive was invented. Beyond that there was nothing.

I didn't remember I had told my wife I felt disoriented, repeated things over and over. "Hey, when did you get your nails done?" "Where did these come from?" — pointing at new shoes. "Why am I here?" — at the hospital admission desk. I had no idea that a neighbor had come downstairs and the two of them took me to the new hospital (the old had actually been destroyed five years ago). The check-in process, CT scan, blood tests, ECG, MRI, X-rays left no memory.

All of this is gone. It was, as they explained, "transient global amnesia": a sudden erasure of short-term memory, without any known cause, without long-term effect, or much likelihood of recurrence.

Looking back, there was no I. A void, vast and pervasive was nearby. There was no center into which experience or memory could be drawn. There was nothing to sustain the continuum of an I even as, to others, I kept acting like myself, chatting, making repeated jokes. For them, I was me. But I had no awareness of this kind of continuum. For me, there was only a large, dark, restless emptiness in which fragments of moments flickered on the surface.

This primordial sea remains still nearby, rolling gently at the edge of experience and memory.

Those so busy with the world's demands rarely see the great precipice always so near. The interwoven nets of earth and sky, of water and wind, of sun and moon and stars, of mountains and

chasms, of mammals, reptiles, insects, birds, and fish, of innumerable invisible life forms, of innumerable kinds of plants, all
weave themselves together into the tapestry of the world. It all
seems so blatant, so obvious, so real, so permanent, so enormous and impersonal. But in old age, the tenuous fragility of
it all, the random play of comings together and fallings apart,
become poignant as our lives come to an end, even as others all
around us are setting out to make new worlds. We, the old, have
seen how a virus may kill millions, a lie may start a war, an echo
may prompt a song, a late arrival may cause a bank to fail, a love
affair to start.

Old, we are ever more vulnerable to small changes. A draft,
a germ, too much something, too little something else, a chair
moved too far away, a response too late. So many small unrave-
lings can bring our life to an end. At the same time, we cannot
imagine stopping, not doing something. And we know, if only
because our bodies now show us, that the smallest parts of life
must be cared for if the large is to go on. Our continuity is not
just a matter of our bodies but of the world. It too must continue. Our lives are inseparable from the lives of all, of everything. We are woven in this vast continuing. Thus, carried on,
we find in our passage constant eruptions of tenderness, flares
of love. Love, it seems, will not let go of us.

* * *

DAISY LOONGKOONAN (1910–2018)

"I am born in the country. When I am gone, it will be lost."
— Daisy Loongkoonan[15]

The river, the Mardoowara, flows for almost 500 miles through
the Northwest Outback of the Australian continent. With its
many branches and tributaries, it is the catchment and water
source for a vast level flood plain of more than 36,000 square
miles. In the parched winter from June through September, the
riverbed almost dries up, leaving deep pools in which the stocks

of fish survive. The rest of the land is semi-arid, desert-like, covered with red dust. In the monsoon rains of summer from December to February, the river rises as much as thirty-five feet in five days; the plains are inundated, and the temperatures rise to more than 100°F. Along the river are dense forests of paperbark and mangrove. On these banks live osprey, spoonbills, storks, egrets, turtles, frogs, pythons; and in the streams, freshwater shrimp, mussels, and crabs flourish. Here also are many kinds of fish: eel, barramundi, catfish, sawfish. On the drier floodplains, amid sparser growths of eucalyptus, dwell kookaburra, pigeons, nightjars, quail, and curlews; they prey on geckos and skinks and capture the monitor lizards which live on mice and moles. This is also the home of wallabies, kangaroos, and possums. At night, bats and flying foxes fill the sky. It is a world, harsh and rich, and, for a long time, had few human inhabitants.

The Nyikina call themselves *Yimardowarra,* "born to the river." They are one of four peoples who have lived along the riverbanks for more than 40,000 years. In all that time, the material, social, and spiritual aspects of their way of living appear to have change little. It was a difficult and often short life. Each group ate what men could kill: fish, mollusks, birds, small animals; and what women could gather: edible tubers, grass seeds, desert plums, grubs, and greens. In the dry season, often there was barely enough food to escape starvation. Yaws, a disease transmitted by close contacts, and insect-borne diseases, especially those causing blindness, were common. Women were treated brutally. The sacrificial rites of scarring, offering blood and front teeth were harsh. They lived unprotected from the elements. Seasonal change, floods, droughts, lightning, hurricanes, fatal or beneficent interactions with animals, birds, reptiles, incursions from neighbors, these were the exterior events which altered the course of tribal and individual existence. People were marked by the land and left marks to note what others might learn from their passage. What we might consider personal identity was a continuous interweaving of land, living beings, ancestors, and sky.

Life required those who dwelt on this land to understand all aspects of its geography, its flora and fauna, and to know how to respond to all the shifting patterns of life around them. These patterns, *kurruwarri,* are transmitted in the songs and laws of the ancestors; they are embodied in rock, water, soil, river-bed, caves, outcroppings; they reverberate in the movements, and cries of living creatures. "The country is an objectification of ancestral subjectivity. Places where significant events took place, where power was left behind, or where ancestors went into the ground and remain — places where ancestral potency is near — are sacred sites."[16]

To live this way demands detailed memory, unwavering attention, and great refinement in sense of smell, sight, sound, taste, and touch. It requires that those who live on the land allow not a hair's breadth of separation between awareness of themselves and awareness of their environment. Time is a single stream, endless, measureless, and coextensive with land and sky, the river, and all who dwell here. Here, all landmarks are personal history, are ancestors.

We who have been born in industrial and post-industrial worlds simply cannot imagine what this means. We assume a life of individual achievement, of personal comfort, of abstract understanding, of control over phenomena and over ourselves. We say, "time is money." Our food and clothing are produced in places and ways we never see. All this for us is normal. We seek independence from all social and familial contingencies; we call this freedom. To those who inhabited Australia since before there was time, our way of life, our minds are almost unknowable.

When the British arrived in the mid-nineteenth century, the Nyikina way of life, this long dream-time from which they emerged and in which they lived for so long, came to an end. They resisted but had no chance. The land was valued monetarily as pasture for sheep and cattle. The river, renamed the Fitzroy, even now is being dammed and channeled for irrigation. People whose ways of life were truly prehistoric now entered history as Aboriginals, as laborers and servants, as exiles in their own land.

Daisy Loongkoonan was born sometime around 1910. Government regulations did not require her parents to register her birth until it was convenient, so the date and even year are not precise. She was born in the Kimberly Region of Western Australia at Mount Anderson near the Mardoowara. Her parents worked on cattle stations in this vast grassland, and from them, Daisy learned the skills necessary for sheep ranching. She also became a cook, particularly adept at baking bread.

Her family's life was more fortunate than that of others. In the months of the wet season, the winter monsoon, she and her parents joined other Nyikina people and went to their land by the river. Every year, they returned to their home ground and their ancient ways of life. As they walked over more than 500 square miles of their ancestral land visiting the tribe's sacred places, she learned the human and non-human history of her people, their songs, their wisdom, their ways of living and surviving, their customary laws which were embedded in every inch and blade of grass of the landscape. She learned to find food plants, to collect medicine, participated in the ceremonies marking the deep changes of life, of birth, menstruation, adulthood, death. They moved their encampment constantly. When she was old, she told a reporter: "Footwalking is the only proper way to learn about country and remember it."[17] "That is how I got to know all the bush tucker [food] and medicine."[18]

She lived the rest of her life working for white ranchers. "I had a good life on the stations," she said, "I had three husbands. Today I am single, and I like to travel about Country and visit Countrymen. I still enjoy footwalking my country, showing the young people how to chase barni [monitor lizards] and catch fish."[19]

By the time she was 95 years old, she had come to embody the traditions of her people and was one of the very last who could speak and understand her ancestral language. She was a revered elder. Nonetheless, her niece Margaret urged her to go to the Manambarra Aboriginal Artists Studio. There, in her great old age, she turned to painting because, as she said, she felt an "urgency" to record her people's sacred places and share her memories of her journeys there. She was confronted by the meaningless void that would be left if her people's world was obliterated. With fervor and determination, she set to work. In the time she had left, she produced almost four hundred paintings.

In her pictures, lines and fields of bright colored dots are arranged in grids to show the domains of plants, reptiles, and animals, and the effect is like vibrant tapestry. The technique is like that in rock and sand painting as well as in ceremonial body ornamentation, "Strictly controlled designs embodying the Dreaming to be enacted are applied to the skin [...] the ochre applied with small daubs in a process that infused or impregnated *kuruwarri* (sacred pattern) with ancestral potency. The painted dots around the *kuruwarri* lines 'push' the *kuruwarri* in and 'draw' the ancestral presence out."[20]

> When [...] Loongkoonan began to paint, her deep understanding burst out like the breaking monsoonal banks of the river so central to her art practice. Her works were metonyms of an encyclopedic knowledge of Nyikina country.[21]

Loongkoonan's paintings are not meant to record a vanished past. The past here cannot be abstracted from or cut out of a continuum of which these paintings are an aerial view. The world that Loongkoonan and other Indigenous Australian artists depict is the real world, the world that never dies and is still unfolding. It continues though we may not see it, though the ability to see it, to live within it, may now be lost.

Many of the patterns which Indigenous Australian artists depict have long been kept secret, sometimes within the tribe but always from outsiders. Revealing them has caused many tribespeople pain. Others, and clearly the artists, reveal these ancient visions in the hope that, as their traditions, lore, and land become less and less available, someone, sometime may yet be inspired to take the painful and demanding path needed to rediscover them.

* * *

As old age nears its end, we are held in an unfamiliar and uninhabitable expanse. There is no turning back. Amid confusion, we sense approaching the definitive clarity of something ending. Finality is close to the surface. And yet, as we look toward the completeness of our end, the warmth of love lingers, holds us back, does not let us go.

We sit in my mother-in-law's room as she wakes up. The old TV in the nurse's station down the hall rattles with metallic laughter. My mother-in-law, smaller, a little pinched, absorbed, not completely aware of us, sits in her bed, holding a black-and-white stuffed cat. For a few minutes, she stares intently at her daughter. Then she looks at me, then looks away. She gazes around the room slowly, back and forth. She smiles gently. She holds the toy cat, stares at it, lifts it up, turns it over and over, watching as if the cat, of its own accord, were drifting through space, as if she herself were that space. She takes her time. Her daughter asks if she ever thinks of her parents. She always spoke of them fondly. But now she looks up sharply. "That got pounded into my head. Pounded." She smacks her fist against her forehead to illustrate, then goes back to watching as her large, expressive hands move the stuffed cat slowly, over, and sideways and over again, as if it were falling, falling through the sky. Bent with arthritis after a long life of handwork, her hands convey her sensitivity and focus. She is not interested in listening or talking; she is exploring an uncharted space that is expanding slowly past familiar boundaries as her mind and body begin to part.

* * *

"M'illumino/D'immenso,"[22] Giuseppe Ungaretti wrote this when he woke in a trench during World War I and suddenly felt engulfed by the vastness of light. On that battlefield, life quickly became death, and death was everywhere. But, for a moment, no boundary separated living and dying: space and light, vision, image, memory. This was not theoretical or mystical. There, poised between continuing and its end, the soldier–poet was, at least momentarily, freed from the preoccupations which hid something larger. In such a moment, he knew what it was to be pinned in the body, in space and time where there is no possible escape; and there, as if in a vast mirror, the expanse of brilliant, overwhelming, and inhuman immensity opened.

* * *

MICHELANGELO BUONARROTI (1475–1564)

Even when quite young, Michelangelo Buonarroti knew that, though highly skilled at drawing and painting, sculpture was his great gift. The uniqueness of his genius was, from his adolescence, recognized by princes and popes; his work and life were thereafter shaped by their ambitions, visions, and whims. Men in power proposed and sponsored his projects, blocked, or altered others, destroyed others yet. He was forced to flee one city and hide in another. He was often beset by hardships, threats, the machinations of rivals, and the wayward finances of capricious patrons. His life, in this regard, was like that of many other artists, though he was successful on a far greater scale.

His inner life, as with most Europeans then, was moved by fear of damnation, yearning for salvation, and the struggle for divine grace. The universal nature of this journey was shared in imagery from the Bible, the life of Christ, the saints, and more recently, articulated in forms derived from classical Greco-Roman myth and sculpture. The latter made possible a more vibrant physicality and greater range of expressive movements. Michelangelo's perceptive and unhesitant application of these possibilities gave his work unique power. For him, the body was the perceivable form of the soul's deepest aspirations as well as its splendor, imprisonment, and anguish. He believed that within every block of stone, divine inspiration stirred, and that God had given him the ability to liberate, it, to bring its form into the world.

By the time he was seventy, Michelangelo had created the masterpieces which secured his renown: the statue of *David* in Florence's Signoria, the ceiling of the Sistine Chapel, the *Pietà* in the Vatican, the designs and statues for the Medici Chapel. Of the sculptures in this chapel, Charles de Tolnay commented: "The mature Michelangelo no longer sees the isolated body as an individual center of energy but seizes the cosmic force that runs through it. The human frame is seen as a receptacle for forces which come to it from outside, pass through it, and afterwards disappear."[23]

Because of his extraordinary gift for revealing the transcendent in physical form, Michelangelo was, at this point in his career, considered the pre-eminent artistic figure in Europe. He had outlived all possible rivals and had an unassailable position in Rome as the architect of Saint Peter's. But in his last thirty years, from when he was sixty until he was almost 90, Michelangelo's work transformed again. In his later life, hope no longer shaped his vision of the cosmos.

In 1537, Michelangelo began work on what was the largest single painting of the time, *The Last Judgment* on the altar wall of the Sistine Chapel. It took four years to complete. Here he depicted the end of all time, past and future when Christ returns to judge the final fate of all people. Unlike the classically beautiful figures he had painted on the chapel ceiling, those in *The Last Judgment* are thick, heavy, almost misshapen. They are weighed down in their flesh as terror, despair, exaltation, and bliss heave and twist them from within. They occupy a space that is violently unstable, an uninhabitable roiling chaos of storm clouds.

At the center, Christ has returned and stands unadorned, naked, muscular, powerful, the son of humankind. Below, the dead rise from their graves. He is not here to teach or give blessings, but to judge. This is the Christ who says in Matthew 24:35: "Heaven and Earth shall pass away, but my word shall not pass away." His face is impassive; his right arm is raised to show the wounds of his crucifixion to those who will be saved; his left hand denies all mercy to those who will be damned. Now, he raises hosts, saints, martyrs, and virtuous from below to his right up into a heaven of eternal bliss. The mass of the sinful and corrupt below him on the left, he casts down into the eternal torments of hell. All originally were portrayed naked since no deceit or concealment can endure this final judgment.

Now prayer has no more influence, and there is no further possibility for forgiveness or compassion. Nothing can be changed. What is done is done. At Christ's side, his mother, Mary, turns away. For sinners, her love and pity have no further place. The world has reached its conclusion. It is the end of time. This is indeed as terrifying a vision as ever presented.

Michelangelo came to look on human fate with a gaze as direct as that with which he looked at everything else. He had contemplated the lustrous beauty of a sorrowing Madonna, the seductive virility of an imperious David, the monumental righteousness of the figures in the Old Testament, the transitory powers of day and night, and so forth. He allowed each to speak through him in its unique way. *The Last Judgment* emerged from Michelangelo's long contemplation of his own final fate and allowed him to draw us, even now, into a vortex where human history has no further possibility and no escape.

The following year, Michelangelo began work on two paintings utterly unlike *The Last Judgment*. These are the frescoes in the adjoining Pauline Chapel: one, *The Conversion of Saint Paul,* the other *The Crucifixion of Saint Peter.* Each is shown in a traditional manner: St. Paul has been thrown from his horse and is blinded by the light of divine illumination; St. Peter is being crucified head down. The saints each confront us, looking out from scenes that have all the appearance of violence but not the feeling. It is all strangely frozen. In the specifics of these depictions of the two saints most central to the establishment of the Roman Catholic Church, "one can sense the absoluteness of the drama enacted between eternal forces and the human being."[24]

But the action in each mural feels remote, painted in delicate colors before vague, pallid landscapes that trail off to the rear. In both, bystanders wander past; they are mostly indifferent or

unaware. Even the soldier about to crucify St. Peter seems unde-
cided. These pictures seem quite detached, as if the journey to
salvation, even at its most extreme, always took place within an
utter stillness untouched by worldly drama. Thus, the extremes
of emotion and suffering presented here are indicated, not rendered. They are signposts in an inner continuity, not an outer
one. The paintings were finished when Michelangelo was 75 and
are his last works of this kind.

For the remaining fourteen years of his life, Michelangelo
spent most of his energy designing and overseeing the construc-
tion of Saint Peter's Cathedral in Vatican City. It was space itself
that concerned him, but he made far less use of the kinds of proportions and musical ratios that other architects were relying on.
Instead, his work was based on a pragmatic and personal vision
to "bring out more forcibly, the cosmic (and perhaps as well the
institutional) aspect to which man is subordinate."[25] Human
beings have their place is these grand spaces, but they are not
exactly free. In this manner, he also undertook the rebuilding of
the Capitoline Hill, the Farnese Palace, and completed, though
in a greatly diminished form, the tomb for his great and tempes-
tuous patron, Pope Julius II.

Michelangelo began his final architectural project in 1563.
Pope Pius IV ordered him to create, within the monumental
Roman ruins of the baths of Diocletian, a church in honor of
a vision of the Virgin Mary surrounded by angels and martyrs. Michelangelo built *Santa Maria degli Angeli e dei Mar-
tiri* out of the bath's huge walls, arches, and apses, and he used
the immense groined vault of the surviving *frigidarium* as the
church's center. The result is a church of unique form, a huge
Greek cross where the transepts are as wide, long, and high as
the nave. It represents, as Paolo Portoghesi put it, "a solemn act
of humility [...] a gesture both utilitarian and religious. [...]
Architecture and existence have become reunified and equal."[26]
Without the need for any imagery or drama, these enormous
volumetric spaces articulate a wordless immensity. They engulf
us in an unimpeded spiritual expanse, as mysterious and deeply

moving as what he created with the dense figuration of the Sistine Chapel. Michelangelo did not live to see its completion.

"To heaven always I am driven; to heaven always I aspire," Michelangelo wrote.[27] Thus, he saw his life and the life of humanity always in this context that was vast and impersonal. All our strivings, passions, and terrors were moments in a larger drama which became complete only in the inescapable and final act of divine judgment. Sculpture, which embodied human longing, imprisonment, and struggle, was as essential to his inner life as contemplation and prayer. Until his last day of life when he was 88 years old, Michelangelo continued carving in stone. He could no longer hold a pen or brush, and his hands caused him constant pain. The sculptures from his last years are unfinished and retain many rough areas which are now part of their effect. His very last sculpture, *The Rondanini Pietà,* columnar in form, arched like a drawn bow, conveys an anguish like that of a soul that cannot get free of its material prison, an intensity of longing that is held by a form that must be forever incomplete.

* * *

Old age makes it clear. We cannot remain anywhere. Our lives will not achieve completion. When we look forward, as if we could glimpse the end of our lives or envision our world being destroyed, it seems we are looking at an expanse for which we have no reference point or measurement, a void. We look to our history and our past to find clues to our future.

In this world, we have always been on the move from place to place to place, as environments change, opportunities emerge, obstacles appear. And we have never been alone. Great flocks of birds, swarms of insects, fish in rivers and seas, reptiles, rodents, herds of deer, moving, moving across this earth we think we can domesticate and own. And the theories, thoughts, desires that create our momentary certainties, they too migrate, as religious conversion, scientific law, artistic taste, architecture, technology, cuisine. Our idea that we are permanent occupants of anywhere in space and time is an illusion that lasts only so long as a complex and mobile combination of environmental, social, and economic conditions allow us to remain.

Our attempts to reduce the incomprehensible dimensions of existence to the scale of our own understanding never stop. Our efforts to contain the ungraspable within our architecture or history, to map it in our spiritual teaching, science, poetry, art, and our narratives, are endless. Our ongoing battle to give ourselves significance amid the completely impersonal unfolding of empty and limitless expanse has no result. Our individuality, our personal endeavors, along with our bodies, will be returned to subatomic dust. We may regard this as a judgment on our egotism and folly, or not. Even the ruins, the records and wreckage we leave behind will disappear without a trace. I sit immobile and look toward the green mountains as a driving rain leaves lines of water trailing on the glass.

In the totality of world and self, past, present, and future, visible and invisible, known and unknown, tangible and intangible, minute and immeasurable, audible and inaudible, all flow together, swirl, twist, mingle, separate, change one into another, dissolve, flow on. We are engulfed and dismembered and reshaped as someone, something we will never see. There is a sharp cramp in my foot and my leg kicks out. For a moment, I forget what I am doing here. In total, this may be stillness or ceaseless movement. Our decision or belief that the ultimate is stillness, or silence, or unknowable is simply an arbitrary moment when we seek one kind of continuity or another. Words and images make our ignorance approachable.

In Hindu and Buddhist traditions, it is maintained that time moves in continuing cycles of increase and decrease, expansion and contraction, waxing and waning. These vast cycles are divided in four eras called *Yugas*. The *Satya-yuga* is the first, the longest and most ideal, a time of inner and outer beauty, purity, and perfection. Desires and their fulfillment are simultaneous. This is said to last 1,728,000 years. Next is the *Tretā-yuga* of 1,296,000 years. In this era, perfection begins to diminish; its luster begins to dim. Longings become goals and paths. In the *Dvāpara-yuga,* lasting 864,000 years, desires, intentions, actions, and social classes become ever more distinct and varied.

Finally, there is our era, the shortest, the *Kali-yuga,* the time of destruction which lasts 432,000 years. Now, desire and the objects of desire are distant. We struggle to unite them, but the results are temporary. Cravings themselves are momentary, marked by anguish, longing, rage. Time accelerates. What one generation believes, the next rejects. The concept of truth itself dies out. Spiritual, moral, and ethical life degenerates. Material advantage becomes the only accepted value. Pollution, corruption, disease, degeneration, and violence fill our minds and poison the world around us. The only virtue that still can be practiced is compassion. We are moving into the end of time. All will end before another cycle begins.

And indeed, we do feel some kind of end approaching. The globe is becoming uninhabitable. The tempo of mass destruction has increased. The last century saw unparalleled slaughter, destruction, dislocation: two world wars, internal slaughters in China, Russia, Cambodia, Uganda, the atom bomb, the Holocaust, and innumerable smaller episodes of mass violence. Dread and unreality pervade the age. This is the old age of the cosmos.[28]

* * *

VYĀSA (1500 BC)

Vyāsa's name means "compiler" in Sanskrit. He was also known as Kṛṣṇadvaipāyana or Vedavyāsa, and he lived around 1500 BC. He was a legendary being, both as author of and actor in two of the greatest works in Indian and world literature. He is the exemplar of all who, in old age, opened a bridge to a completely new way of seeing.

Vyāsa's earliest achievement was to have edited the ancient Vedas and divided them into sections so they would be accessible for ordinary people. Then he wrote or assembled the greatest of all epics, the *Mahābhārata.* Finally, in his very old age, he composed a very different kind of book, the *Bhāgavata Purāṇa*. This is a long text providing a pathway for human beings at the end of time to move from history and enter the realm of the gods.

The Mahābhārata was a record of events in the eon that immediately preceded this final era in which we now live. It recounted the fatal struggles between two clan branches, both said to be descended from Vyāsa's own grandchildren. Vyāsa intervened at many points in the action of *The Mahābhārata* and thus was a progenitor of the principal actors, an actor himself, and the author of this great collective history of humanity. This vast compilation, filled with innumerable accounts of love, rivalry, fidelity, jealousy, war, and complex family evolution, marked the end of the *Dvāpara-yuga*.

After Vyāsa completed the *Mahābhārata,* he was exhausted and in despair. The *Kali-yuga,* the age of darkness and destruction had begun, but Vyāsa did not die. With his four disciples and his son, Shuka, he retreated deep into the forest of Daṃḍaka. He realized that his ordering of the Vedas would only benefit the priesthood, and the *Mahābhārata* would only provide people with worldly understanding; neither would it free humanity from the darkness, greed, and confusion of the *Kali-yuga*. This required a very different kind of teaching. So, Vyāsa meditated, reflecting on all that had come before and all that would come afterward. Old age had stripped him of any belief that humanity controlled its fate. His mind moved between sleep and dream and hovered beyond life and death. He saw the *Kali-yuga* come to an end.

The world and all the forms of consciousness it supported dissolved into a roiling sea of atoms split apart, particles of momentary awareness, light waves without origin or end, flickering thought forms without reference. He saw wave upon wave of transitory shapes, figures, congruences, dissonances, attractions, repulsions, light and dark, vibrant, inert, multi-colored, colorless, warm, cold.

Vyāsa felt himself dissolving, as human, as place, as reference point, in the surface of the Pralaya, the Sea of Dreams. He was dissolving back into the primordial moment before awareness began and after existence ended. He saw the Pralaya rising through the minds of beings in the dark age as cosmic amnesia washed away their learning, accomplishments, skills, wisdom, their memories altogether. Vyāsa floated in this luminous, lightless void, this infinite expanse, neither space nor time. Here he saw the last dark age dissolve, and a new cosmos emerge. In this infinite expanse, he entered universe after universe, world after world, being after being, as each dissolved to reemerge in different form.

Over and over, he saw, deep within the Sea of Dreams, a faint form coalesce. A dark blue light, glowing softly in the depth of the sea, slowly became the form of a baby glowing like a sapphire, asleep and dreaming, cradled, and rocking in the coils of an immense green serpent. Vyāsa saw emerging from this sleeping baby's navel, rising like a dream, a long emerald stem that gradually rose to the surface of the Pralaya. Over centuries, from its green calyx a vast thousand-petalled pink lotus of shining light unfolded. From its pistil and stamen, a delirious scent of love filled the air. On the golden anthers swaying at the center of this lotus in full bloom, the cosmos, fresh, new, and pure, began again, just as it had done thousands of times before and would do thousands of times again. Patterns and chaos alternated on both minute and cosmic scales. The radiant lotus petals fluttered softly, and music, inseparable from silence, filled the whole of space. Thus, Vyāsa experienced primordial mind, immense, luminous, all-pervasive.

Then, burning like a rainbow of suns in unmeasurable time, Vyāsa saw goddesses and gods blaze across space. Brahmā and his retinue, Viṣṇu, his avatars, and devotees, Śiva and his lovers, emerged in their golden chariots, riding through the shining air. He saw their loves and battles and heard their wisdom and their songs, saw their beauty, their caprices, their paradises. He sat with sages and danced with devotees. He heard all the worlds speaking, singing, going to war, doing business, farming, weaving, gambling, drinking, feasting, making love, giving birth, starving, stealing, dying. He saw how this world, too, would end.

As Vyāsa aged, all feeling, yearning, understanding, memory, appetites, visions became concentrated in his shrinking body. He was filled with the incommunicable intensity of boundless love. Thus, the words of the *Purāṇas* covered the surface of his mind like the iridescent swirling on a soap bubble.

Vyāsa saw that just as a mayfly's life is a human day, a human life is an instant in the life of a deity. He saw that all living beings were composed of trillions of other kinds of beings, each with its own lifespan. He saw millions of invisible ghosts and spirits each caught in its own fate. He saw that the living and the dead walked side by side without knowing it, that innumerable civilizations of insects, rodents, birds, animals, reptiles, fish, fungi, and trees coexisted ignorant of each other within the human realm. There were immeasurable kinds of existences moving through life and death, unseen, unheard, unbeknownst to each other.

Vyāsa spun together hundreds of thousands of moments in tens of thousands of strands. He wove *The Bhāgavata Purāṇa* so that those in the age of destruction could find their way to a life of passionate devotion, undistorted, and uncorrupt. Here, for the first time, were written in one place the lives and deeds of the gods in their celestial domains, the accounts of the sages who bowed down to learn from them, and the history of all humanity's deeds. Thus, these things were not lost. And in these texts, devotion offered paths of liberation. This was Vyāsa's final gift to a cosmos that would soon destroy itself.

Vyāsa recited this text to his son, Shuka, whose name means "parrot," and who had the ability to remember and repeat everything he ever heard. At that time, a messenger came to Vyāsa, telling him that King Parīkṣit, last of the Pāṇḍava kings, the victors in the *Mahābhārata,* was sitting by the river Ganges, waiting for his life to end. Vyāsa sent Shuka to recite the *Purāṇa* to the dying lord. Thus did the one who originated the epic seek to liberate the last of the family whose story it was. Shuka went to King Parīkṣit as he sat dying. The king had no more power, no control over anything or anyone anymore. His wishes and desires meant nothing. Now he could only sit and wait for death, as the Ganges flowed timelessly before him. He listened as Shuka began his recitation with these words:

> This *Purāṇa-Sun*
> has risen for those who have been blinded by
> the age of *Kali*.[29]

For seven days and nights without interruption, Shuka then recited the *Bhāgavata Purāṇa,* and King Parīkṣit listened without distraction. Others nearby wrote down the words. When the reading neared its end, Shuka sang:

> Time, without end, is the destroyer.
> Time, without beginning, is the creator.
> Immutable, creating beings through other
> beings.
> He destroys through death.
> even the Lord of death.[30]

And he concluded:

> O king, now do not fear death.
> Just as when a vase shatters,
> Space that was within it does not change.
> But merges with space
>
> When a log burns,
> Heat dissipates in air.
> When a river joins the sea,
> Water is inseparable from its vast expanse.
>
> Birth, Life, Death are moments, words.
> In old age and death, they lose their meaning
> Completely.[31]

When all the *Bhāgavata Purāṇa* had been read to him, King Parīkṣit, the last of his celebrated lineage, died. There was nothing to perpetuate or to end. He let himself go. His devotion, his love, his gratitude could go no further. The universe was exhausted.

Vyāsa remained in his forest dwelling and waited for his son's return. But Shuka had become a solitary wanderer, and they never met again. Vyāsa, grieved at being parted from this child he loved so dearly; he cried out, "Oh my son." The trees, into whose deep shadows Shuka had vanished, whispered. Vyāsa listened but could not understand. Nothing after that moment of incomprehension is known about the person we call Vyāsa.

It is in the smallest moment, the shortest silence, the tiniest flicker, the most minute gap that the end truly ends. And it is in that same miniscule caesura that beginning begins. And only in that single instant do they meet and part.

* * *

Now, in the warm shallow valley before the yellowing foothills, now, around the barking dog, now before the smell of burning toast, now beneath the cold soles of feet, a sleeping wife's slight snore in the dark bedroom, space expands in these articulations. Space here inseparable from all forms of awareness but never touched by them. A space that is itself at a slight distance from that which appears within it.

The tangible and intangible, the unknown and the known, the living and those who live only now in memory, appear in an expanse that stirs slightly, withdraws, moves forward, expands above, below, in all directions side to side. Alive, continuing.

Moving outward, on, it absorbs the "I," the "it," the "you," the "they," the "we," the "is" and "was" and "will be." It is expanse, shimmering, boundless, not reliant on sense or experience or awareness of any kind. Not a thing. I appear and disappear and appear and disappear and there is no continuum or resting place outside or within.

There is indeed a secret expanse which we, the old, find ourselves inhabiting. The body in its final time is both intensely claustrophobic and completely empty. Nothing is fixed. The losses are painful, but now there is less here, less there, less now, less then. The absence of so many true friends and lovers is a constant sorrow, but frequently it seems they are close by. It is love and understanding still linking us. We are still in the rolling terrain where we look for ways to reach this and avoid that.

The grasses, dry, almost golden, their tassels bright in the evening sun, now bring me back to the moment when I first came here and stepped out onto a path which branched out and became many, became my life. I met a teacher from Tibet and this meeting led to other teachers, other friends, marriages, fatherhood, other kinds of studies, different kinds of jobs, teaching, writing, learning lofty things and humble ones. I became learned and foolish, was arrogant and humiliated, fell in love more than once, had a bad marriage, a wonderful marriage, learned betrayal from both sides, knew good fortune and bad, and, bit by bit, knew the end of all those things, and other things beginning.

And now I look at the gilded tawny fields I first saw fifty years ago, and they are the same. A hot summer evening. It is slightly humid but very clear, and I feel that first moment, that tingle of desire, that warmth of beginning, of being drawn onward as the sun which has been so very hot today drifts behind the dark mountain ridge, and pale clouds rise, and the soil cools leaving the smell of heat and growing and drying.

I feel the long-ago beginning on this, the same ground as now I feel the end. Tenderness and gratitude. It really is love. And even if it was an illusion or is going to end in two seconds and will be forgotten everywhere forever as if it never was, this love is real, and it is complete.

VI

Afterword

In our old age, we finally know that the world emerging around us and within us was always unknown. We move cautiously. This unsought state of clarity does not conform, even less now than before, to our desires. A world is emerging through us; perhaps despite us. It passes through our body and mind and reshapes our existing framework to make its way. What is coming into being does not accommodate us. We do not have the power to change this. We are becoming strangers, exiles in the world we have made, becoming aliens to ourselves.

We have accomplished and not accomplished things we set out to do. Many of the people who would have known what we struggled to attain and might have had some idea of what it took for us to do what we did, and what it also might mean in the larger world, all have gone. And their worlds too.

The complex of minor pains stops occasionally. But they return, and I am increasingly aware of weakness, an impending inability to do simple things, things I always assumed I would. There is an approaching boundary, a glass wall cutting me off. One the other side, there is the intensity of life going on, futures being made; the intensity of physical passion where lovers feel so incandescent, as they slide their hands down into the back of each other's pants, they think they are invisible to those walking behind, an old man and woman who have not forgotten, even if now in aging bodies, things express themselves differently. This love, this continuing we do not control.

Tonight, I am more alone than I would have imagined, but, strangely, not lonely. The bright sunset swirls and glimmers in the darkening sky of early evening. This dissolves as I am wandering across a city college campus. I'm killing time. What do they teach here? It's not my world. It's more abstract. I am leaning forward to lessen the tension in my spine.

The core of discomfort cannot be assuaged. Continuous pain brings with it a feeling of the world fading, becoming more pale, delicate in this first lovely spring evening of the year. Only a little cool, pale yellow light, faint orange on the brick walls; it looks like there should be the smell of dogwood, but there is not. The slightest crescent of a moon ascends from the horizon.

Soon, sitting in the semi-darkness in the back of the auditorium, the dancers dance, the musicians play, the pain is less. Nothing is expected of me, even wanted. Pain will return when I stand up. I read:

A Buddha says,
My body,
Like space,
forms
like a water-moon.
…

[…] A buddha's body is like space. Space is like a Buddha's body, so any thing — earth, world, appearance — is space in person. Like water. Like all phenomena — they're a buddha's body. Like water. Like a moon.[1]

The end, completely unknowable, is always close. An invisible line that cuts across everything, slices invisibly and inaudibly through experience within and without. Life is always on the edge of loss, of transformation into something unknowable, of complete disappearance. But it is a continuous acknowledgment.

Life is continuing intensely. Right now, I fall into the light of a sunset.

IGOR STRAVINSKY (1882–1971)

In an interview published in *The New York Times* in June 1966, Igor Stravinsky, then the most famous composer in the Western world, discussed the rigors of his prolonged and painful sicknesses. He said:

> I suffer, too, as never before and as I have never admitted, from my musical isolation, being obliged to live now at a detached and strictly mind level of exchange with younger people who profess to wholly different belief systems. I am also, and for the first time in my life, bothered by a feeling of loneliness for my generation. All of my contemporaries are dead. It is not so much old friends or individuals, nevertheless, and certainly not the mentality of my generation, that I regret, but the background as a whole.[2]

Sometime later, I experienced what was undoubtedly the most fortunate of many memorable times in the concert hall. My father had been given tickets to the dress rehearsal and world premiere of Stravinsky's *Requiem Canticles*. He knew I was far more interested than he in such things and kindly gave them to me. Stravinsky was a great presence in my life. His conversations with Robert Craft in the *New York Review of Books* sparkled with a range of references and depth of experiences, shaping my sense of what an artist or a person active in the world could be.

As I recall, the dress rehearsal took place at around 11 AM. Except for the warmly lit stage, the large, boxy auditorium was dark and chilly. The ensemble and chorus were waiting on the stage. The conductor, Robert Craft, Stravinsky's assistant, friend and, in some ways, muse, had not yet arrived. Most of the music students and faculty were scattered in clumps throughout the hall. Because my musical education was limited, I felt quite shy so found a place out of view in a side balcony.

The acoustics there were not the best, but I could see Stravinsky, swathed in white scarf and tan overcoat, tiny, bald, and pale, frail like a newly hatched bird. His wife sat next to him on one side, on the other, an empty seat, then a man who frequently leaned over and commented as Stravinsky looked at the score lit by a stand light on a table in front of him. The instrumentalists were arranging themselves, but there was perhaps less banter than there might have been. The people in the audience were almost silent. Everyone was very aware that this was most likely, as so it turned out to be, the composer's last major piece. Stravinsky had had his first stroke ten years earlier, and although he had continued to compose and conduct, strokes continued to weaken him.

Robert Craft, self-effacing in gray suit, black horn-rimmed glasses, came in from the rear of the hall, walked to the front and sat with the Stravinsky and his wife, leaned past her to listen to the composer. There was an easy intimacy amongst them. The auditorium was silent as the two men talked quietly. Finally, Craft stepped up on stage, said a few things to the players, and the rehearsal began with the urgent plaintive strings in the opening section of the piece. I was aware of hearing something few had ever heard before and felt myself entering a new world.

Stravinsky's frequently published conversations with Robert Craft were a stream of stories about the greatest artists, musicians, and writers of the twentieth century, all of whom he had known, at least in passing, accounts of often quite recondite books, plays, operas, music, poetry, art works, and all seasoned with his acerbic repartee. As a conductor and sometimes lecturer, Stravinsky traveled constantly, and thus had met everyone of cultural significance everywhere. He could be amusing and cutting about all this. He was himself an intersection of many critical vectors in twentieth-century culture. It was hard to escape the sense that Stravinsky was not just the representative of one culture or another, but that he embodied culture itself. He was so dazzling and complete in this role, that it was easy to forget that he exemplified another aspect of twentieth-century life; he was always an exile.

He had been forced to leave Russia; his property, his bank accounts, and his copyrights had been confiscated. He lived in many parts of Europe. He was forced to escape the Nazis in Paris, and seek shelter first in Los Angeles, then New York. Though there was really no time in which he was not one of the most famous people in the world, he had to make a place for himself anew everywhere he went. He did not have the security of home ground. This also led to a reputation for being extremely mercenary, even if always witty. A friend who knew him well, gave him, as a joke, a copy of the US Tax Code for Christmas. He called a few days later to see what Stravinsky thought. In his thick accent, he murmured, "My darling, I wept on every page."

Beginning in his early seventies, and influenced by his new friend Craft, Stravinsky made a radical change in his compositional methods and began using serial composition techniques. This brought about a great rejuvenation in Stravinsky's composing life. Many of the major pieces from this time were based on Christian and Hebrew liturgies, even if perhaps the best-known work from that time was *Agon,* written as a ballet for his friend, compatriot, and near-contemporary, Georges Balanchine. This challenging, confrontational, and seductively strict piece marked a very different kind of Stravinsky. Balanchine's highly abstract choreography changed the landscape of ballet. At this time, he also composed several pieces in memory of deceased friends and colleagues, "necrologies" as he called them. Stravinsky's spirituality as well as his sense of loss were deep, and, except in his music, infrequently made public. All these pieces echoed the austere faith of an almost forgotten time. Perhaps his deep loncliness gave a particular urgency to create such vital linkages between his vanished world and the one in which he found himself. But it was also a deep devotion and unceasing love that drove him to continue, revealing new harmonies, rhythms, and resonances, illuminating the world from which soon he would depart.

The evening of the première, I was at the back under the balcony. Many famous composers, writers, and intellectuals were there, but the person I remember was Robert Oppenheimer.

He wore a tuxedo, was gaunt, his face very flushed and frozen in a kind of terrible anguish. He seemed so deeply pained that those who did not know and greet him, looked away. It had been widely reported that when he witnessed the first atom bomb test, Oppenheimer found a line from the *Mahaābhārata* surfacing in his mind: "Now I am become Death, the destroyer of worlds." He had been essential in creating the most destructive weapon ever seen and looked like a man burned to the core.

The audience settled quickly, and, after some other pieces which I no longer remember, *Requiem Canticles* began with the prelude, hushed, urgent strings, and unfolded through nine sections, with a great variety of rhythmic devices, melodic transformations, and combinations of instrumental and choral settings that made the relatively short but deeply moving work seem expansive and vast. It seemed to rise out of a distant darkness and carry us on the subliminal pulse of a hidden stream. Craft would later write about how Stravinsky had "discovered' the musical material from which the piece evolved, and indeed it progresses with a kind of natural-seeming logic and vitality. Perhaps most striking for me, were the beginning, the end, and the "Libera Me" with the chorus singing and speaking simultaneously, somewhat in the manner Stravinsky used in his choral piece *Threni*. But the essential feeling of the whole requiem, even with its many complex and subtle effects, was simplicity, as if at the center of every note, chord and phrase was a muted cry of loss. At the conclusion, the audience was silent, as had been requested in the program, but suddenly Oppenheimer leapt to his feet applauding. The audience quickly followed in a prolonged standing ovation. Later, I read that Oppenheimer had this piece played at his funeral.

Stravinsky wrote other pieces after *Requiem Canticles,* but they were short chamber works. Soon, he could no longer travel or conduct; even receiving guests became burdensome. So, it is remarkable and inspiring that being so ill, Stravinsky could still reach deeply into his being, his heritage, and his longing to produce this last great piece as well as those afterwards.

Stravinsky's last works have a severe beauty that remains always haunting. Clearly, he knew he could not live much longer. The chords, their progressions, their movement forward resonate with an inner clarity, a deep stillness. Even just remembering them, it's easy to imagine being in the cold vaulted nave of an abandoned Romanesque church, seated near a pale limestone column. There's one melodic fragment, one sequence, one confluence of instruments and voices, one rhythm and then another. They shimmer in the still air. Each changes our sense of what went before. Feeling death stirring nearby, the future is void; the past and the present are luminous, momentary, continuous, completely new. There is so much here. I am old, and, within this, cannot long remain.

It is just as Bashō wrote near the end of his life:

The Moon and the Sun are eternal travelers. Even the years wander on. A lifetime adrift in a boat, or in old age leading a tired horse into the years, every day is a journey, and the journey itself is home. From the earliest time there have always been some who perished along the road.[3]

Notes

PREFACE

1. Henry David Thoreau, *Walden* (Viking Penguin Books, 1983), 217.
2. Marcel Proust, *Time Regained,* trans. Andreas Mayor, Terence Kilmartin, and D.J. Enright (Modern Library, 2002), 357.
3. Lewis Lockwood, *Beethoven: The Music and the Life* (W.W. Norton & Co., 2003), 349.
4. Ibid., 363.
5. Ibid., 266.
6. Ibid., 353.
7. Ibid., 354.
8. Ibid., 357.
9. "Beethoven and Rossini," *Popular Beethoven,* https://www.popularbeethoven.com/beethoven-and-rossini/.
10. Ludwig van Beethoven, *Letters, Journals, Conversations,* ed. and trans. Michael Hamburger (Thames & Hudson, 1951), 177–78.
11. Fredric Jameson, "Postmodernism, or the Cultural Logic of Late Capitalism," *New Left Review* 146 (1984): 58–59. Parts of this section were published in *Common Dreams,* September 23, 2024 as "A Few Thoughts on This Admission: I

Am Old," https://www.commondreams.org/opinion/our-old-age.

I – BODY

1. William Empson, "To an Old Lady," in *The Complete Poems,* ed. John Haffenden (Allen Lane, 2000), 24.
2. Simone de Beauvoir, *The Second Sex,* trans. Constance Borde and Sheila Malovaney-Chevallier (Vintage, 2010), 747, cited in Sue Zemka, "Descent, Spirit, Heart, Senses," in *Literature and the Senses,* eds. Annette Kern-Stähler and Elizabeth Robertson (Oxford University Press, 2023), 70.
3. Maurice Merleau-Ponty, "Exploring the World of Perception," *The French Cultural Hour,* French National Radio, October 16, 1948, cited and translated in Zemka, "Descent, Spirit, Heart, Senses," 71.
4. Adapted from Milarepa, *The Hundred Thousand Songs of Milarepa,* trans. Garma C.C. Chang (University Books, 1962), 554.
5. André Gregory, *This Is Not My Memoir* (Farrar, Strauss and Giroux, 2020), 176.
6. Thomas Bernhard, *Old Masters,* trans. Ewald Osers (Penguin Books, 2020), cited in Nordbert Wolf, *I, Titian,* trans. Ishbel Flett (Prestel Verlag, 2006), 22.
7. Erwin Panofsky, *Meaning in the Visual Arts* (Anchor Books, 1955), 147.
8. Giorgio Vasari, *Lives of the Painters, Sculptors and Architects,* vol. 4, trans. A.B. Hinds (Dent, 1963), 209, also cited in Huong Vu, "The Reflection of Age and Beauty in Titian's Late Style," ed. Miray Eroglu, *Canvas,* https://www.canvasjournal.ca/read/the-reflection-of-age-and-beauty-in-titians-late-style.
9. Cited in David Rosand, "Titian and the Critical Tradition," in *Titian: His World and His Legacy,* ed. David Rosand (Columbia University Press, 1982), 24.
10. Zbigniew Herbert. "Apollo and Marsyas," in *The Collected Poems,* trans. Alissa Valles (HarperCollins, 2002), 164.

11. John Steer, *Venetian Painting: A Concise History* (Thames and Hudson, 1970), 138–44.
12. Bernard Berenson, S*unlight and Twilight, from Diaries 1947–58* (Harcourt Brace, 1963), 83.
13. From the *Llywarch Saga* (mid-9th c. Wales). See Joseph P. Clancy, *Welsh Medieval Poems* (Four Courts Press, 2001), 89.
14. Liliane Pizzichinni, *The Blue Hour* (Norton & Co., 2009), 31.
15. Ibid, 221.
16. Jean Rhys, *Wide Sargasso Sea* (Norton & Co., 1966), 130.
17. Thomas Marcus Beardmore, "The Voice of Jean Rhys_0001.wmv," *YouTube,* November 17, 2012, https://www.youtube.com/watch?v=UN_6xJJNphY.
18. Plato, *Symposium,* 207d–208b, cited in Helen Small, *The Long Life* (Oxford University Press, 2007), 31.
19. Elaine Scarry, *The Body in Pain* (Oxford University Press, 1985), 28.
20. Maurice Merleau-Ponty, "Cézanne's Doubt," in *Sense and Nonsense,* trans. Hubert L. Dreyfus and Patricia Allen Dreyfus (Northwestern University Press, 1964), 18.
21. Alex Danchev, ed. and trans., *The Letters of Paul Cézanne* (Getty Museum, 2013), 347.
22. Paul Cézanne, "Letters from Paul Cézanne to Emile Bernard," *Art History Project,* https://www.arthistoryproject.com/artists/paul-cezanne/letters-from-paul-cezanne-to-emile-bernard/.
23. Maurice Merleau-Ponty, "Eye and Mind," in *The Merleau-Ponty Aesthetics Reader: Philosophy and Painting,* ed. Galen A. Johnson (Northwestern Univesoty Press, 1993), 141.
24. Bernard Dorival, *Paul Cézanne,* trans. H.H.A. Thackthwaite (Continental Book Center, 1948), 101.
25. Merleau-Ponty, "Eye and Mind," 149.

II – LINKAGE

1. Ford Madox Ford, "The Lay of the Land," cited in Charles Hallisey, "The Secret of a Woman of Ninety: Rethinking the Very Long Life," in *Rethinking the Human,* eds. J. Michelle Molina and Donald K. Swearer (Center for the Study of World Religions, Harvard Divinity School, 2010), 57.
2. Jerome Silbergeld, "Chinese Concepts of Old Age and Their Role in Chinese Painting, Painting Theory, and Criticism," *Art Journal* 46, no. 2 (1987): 103.
3. Cited in ibid., 104.
4. Cited in ibid., 105.
5. Cited in ibid.
6. Cited in ibid., 106.
7. Cited in ibid.
8. Cited in ibid.
9. Coluga Pictures, "Are You A Turner Or A Constable Man- David Hockney outtake 23/80," *YouTube,* June 13, 2020, https://www.youtube.com/watch?v=mMNpqLk9CjM.
10. Simone de Beauvoir, *Old Age,* trans. Patrick O'Brien (Penguin Books, 1977), 604.
11. Rabindranath Tagore, *Gitanjali,* available on *Project Gutenberg,* https://www.gutenberg.org/cache/epub/7164/pg7164-images.html, no. 84.
12. Ibid., no. 100.
13. W.B. Yeats, Introduction to ibid., section II.
14. Rabindranath Tagore, *Rabindranath Tagore on Art and Aesthetics* (Orient Longmans, 1961), 110.
15. Ibid., 98.
16. Ibid., 99.
17. Ibid., 111.
18. Rabindranath Tagore, *The Meaning of Art* (Lalit Kala Akademi, 1983), 6.
19. Ibid., 5.
20. Simone de Beauvoir, cited in Hallisey, "The Secret of a Woman of Ninety," 59.

21. Aristotle, *Rhetoric*, 2.13, 1389b–1390a, cited in Small, *The Long Life*, 61–62.

22. Philip Larkin,"The Old Fools," *All Poetry*, https://allpoetry.com/The-Old-Fools.

23. Cited in George Bornstein, "W.B. Yeats's Poetry of Aging." *The Sewanee Review* 120, no. 1 (2012): 61.

24. Leoš Janáček, *Leoš Janáček's Uncollected Essays on Music*, ed. and trans. Mirka Zemanová (Marion Boyars Publishers, 1989), 69.

25. Ibid., 47.

26. Mirka Zemanová, *Janáček: A Composer's Life* (Northeastern University Press, 2002), 154.

27. Ibid., 116.

28. Ibid., 117.

29. Ibid., 118.

30. Ibid., 117.

31. Marcel Proust, *In Search of Lost Time*, vol. 6: *Time Regained*, trans. Andreas Mayor and Terence Kilmartin, rev. D.J. Enright (Modern Library, 2002), 415.

32. Ibid., 417.

33. Stéphane Mallarmé, "The Impressionists and Edouard Manet," cited in Margaret Werth, "Mallarmé and Impressionism in 1876," *Nonsite* 27 (2019), https://nonsite.org/mallarme-and-impressionism-in-1876/.

34. André Dombrowski, "Impressionism and the Industrialization of Time," *Yale University Press*, January 5, 2024, https://yalebooks.yale.edu/2024/01/05/impressionism-and-the-industrialization-of-time/.

35. Kenneth Clark, "The Artist Grows Old," *Daedalus* 135, no. 1 (2006): 81.

36. "Georges Clemenceau and Claude Monet," *Georges Clemenceau's House*, https://www.maison-de-clemenceau.fr/en/discover/the-many-facets-of-georges-clemenceau/georges-clemenceau-and-claude-monet.

37. Cited in Robert L. Herbert, "The Decorative and the Natural in Monet's Cathedrals," in *Aspects of Monet: A Sympo-*

sium on the Artist's Life and Times, eds. John Rewald and
Frances Weitzenhoffer (Abrams, 1984), 175.

38. Ernst Jünger, *A German Officer in Occupied Paris: The War
Journals,* 1941–1945, trans. Thomas S. Hansen and Abby J.
Hansen (Columbia University Press, 2019), 335.

39. Michel de Certeau, *The Practice of Everyday Life,* trans.
Steven Rendall (University of California Press, 1988), 103.

40. Ibid., 106.

41. Ibid., 108.

42. Maurice Merleau-Ponty, *The Visible and the Invisible,* trans.
Alphonso Lingis (Northwestern University Press, 1968),
248–49. Emphasis original.

43. Roy Scranton, *Learning to Die in the Anthropocene:
Reflections on the End of a Civilization* (City Lights Books,
2015), 107.

44. Cao Zhi [Ts'ao Chih], "The Ruins of Lo Yang," trans.
Arthur Waley, in *One Hundred and Seventy Chinese Poems*
(Knopf, 1919), 86–87.

III – WAITING

1. Wallace Stevens, "The Well Dressed Man with a Beard," in
Collected Poems of Wallace Stevens (Alfred A. Knopf, 1971),
247.

2. Sigmund Freud, "A Disturbance of Memory on the
Acropolis (1936)," in *The Standard Edition of the Complete
Psychological Works of Sigmund Freud,* vol. XXII: *New
Introductory Lectures on Psycho-Analysis and Other Works
(1932–1936),* trans. James Strachey with Anna Freud
(Hogarth Press, 1964), 241. Emphasis original. A previous
version of this section appeared as "Adrift," *Berfrois,*
September 19, 2022, https://www.berfrois.com/2022/09/
douglas-penicks-memories-of-memory/.

3. Ibid., 248.

4. Pierre-Albert Jourdan, *The Straw Sandals: Selected Prose
and Poetry,* trans. John Taylor (Chelsea Editions, 2011), 233.
A previous version of this section appeared as "A Poet In

Passing: Pierre-Albert Jourdan," *Berfrois,* March 8, 2022, https://www.berfrois.com/2022/03/douglas-penick-on-pierre-albert-jourdan/.

5. Ibid., 281.
6. Ibid., 285.
7. Ibid., 297.
8. Ibid., 313.
9. Ibid., 319.
10. *Mencius* or *Mengzi,* 3A/4, cited in Michael Puett, "The Haunted World of Humanity: Ritual Theory from Early China," in *Rethinking the Human,* eds. J. Michelle Molina and Donald K. Swearer (Center for the Study of World Religions, Harvard Divinity School, 2010), 95.
11. Ibid., 96–97.
12. Ruth Hayden, *Mrs Delany: Her Life and Her Flowers* (British Museum, 1980), 20.
13. Ibid.
14. Molly Peacock, *The Paper Garden* (Bloomsbury, 2012) 4.
15. Augusta Waddington Hall Llanover, ed., *The Autobiography and Correspondence of Mary Granville, Mrs. Delany,* vol. 1, second series (Richard Bentley, 1862), 418 (February 23, 1772). Emphasis original.
16. Ibid., 469 (October 4, 1772).
17. Hayden, *Mrs Delany,* 132–33.
18. Peacock, *The Paper Garden,* 7.
19. Ibid.
20. Ibid., 9.
21. Cited in "Mary Granville Delany: She Invented the Art of Mixed Media Collage at Age 71," *Later Bloomer,* https://laterbloomer.com/mary-granville-delany/.
22. Peacock, *The Paper Garden,* 12.
23. Stéphane Mallarmé, *The Book,* trans. Sylvia Gorelick (Exact Change 2018), ix.
24. Ibid.
25. Adapted from Stéphane Mallarmé, *Un coup de dés,* trans. Anthony Hartley (Penguin, 1965), 214–34.
26. Arakawa Shūsaku, personal communication.

27. James S. Ackerman, *Palladio* (Penguin Books, 1966), 16.
28. Ibid.
29. Rudolph Witkower, *Architectural Principles in the Age of Humanism* (Norton, 1971), 132.
30. Giorgio Vasari, *Lives of the Painters, Sculptors and Architects,* vol. 4, trans. A.B. Hinds (Dent, 1963), 235.
31. Guido Beltramini, *The Private Palladio,* trans. Irena Murray and Eric Ormsby (Lars Müller, 2008), 61.
32. Ibid., 50.
33. Ackerman, *Palladio,* 156.
34. Ibid., 158.

IV – DOMAINS OF LOSS

1. Dogen, "Thirty-seven Pieces of Dharma," in *Abruptly Dogen,* ed. and trans. Kidder Smith (punctum books, 2020), 158.
2. Richard Wilhelm and Cary F. Baynes, trans., *The I Ching or Book of Changes* (Princeton University Press, 1950), 231.
3. Ibid., 694.
4. Atul Gawande, *Being Mortal: Illness, Medicine and What Matters in the End* (Profile Books, 2014), 9.
5. Walter Benjamin, "Robert Walser," trans. Rodney Livingston, in *Selected Writings,* vol. 2, part 1: *1927–1930,* eds. Michael W. Jennings, Howard Eiland, and Gary Smith (Harvard University Press, 1999), 258. A previous version of this section appeared as "A Wanderer," *Berfrois,* May 21, 2021, https://www.berfrois.com/2021/05/douglas-penick-on-robert-walser/.
6. Robert Walser, *Looking at Pictures,* trans. Susan Bernofksy, Lydia Davis, and Christopher Middleton (New Directions, 2015), 141.
7. Cited in Wayne Macauley, "Nobody Should Be Afraid of His Little Bit of Weirdness: A Sideways Look at Robert Walser," *Syndey Review of Books,* October 24, 2014, https://sydneyreviewofbooks.com/essays/nobody-should-be-

afraid-of-his-little-bit-of-weirdness-a-sideways-look-at-robert-walser.

8. Robert Walser, *Microscripts,* trans. Susan Bernofsky (New Directions, 2010), 107.
9. Centers for Disease Control, "About Dementia," August 17, 2024, https://www.cdc.gov/alzheimers-dementia/about/.
10. "2020 Alzheimer's Disease Facts and Figures," *Alzheimer's & Dementia* 16, no. 3 (2020): 398.
11. See also Douglas Penick, "Gateways in Clouds: Stepping into Confusion," *Tricycle* (Spring 2022), https://tricycle.org/magazine/dementia-buddhism/.
12. Louis-Auguste Blanqui, *Eternity by the Stars: An Astronomical Hypothesis,* trans. Frank Chouraqui (Contramundum Press, 2013), 146. A previous version of this section appeared as "Blanqui," *Berfrois,* January 28, 2022, https://www.berfrois.com/2022/01/douglas-penick-on-louis-auguste-blanqui/.
13. Ibid., 149.
14. Kidder Smith with Mike Zhai, trans., *Li Bo Unkempt* (punctum books, 2022), 21.
15. Maurice Merleau-Ponty, "Exploring the World of Perception," *The French Cultural Hour,* French National Radio, October 16, 1948, cited and translated in Zemka, "Descent, Spirit, Heart, Senses," 83.
16. Eduardo Kohn, *How Forests Think: Toward an Anthtropology Beyond the Human* (University of California Press, 2013), 195.
17. Ibid.
18. Ibid., 188. The phrase cited is from C.S. Pierce.
19. Ibid., 176–77.
20. Claude Lévi-Strauss, *Wild Thought,* trans. Jeffrey Mehlman and John Leavittt (Chicago University Press, 2021), 247.
21. Alexander Dreier, *The Brain Is a Boundary: A Journey in Poems to the Borderlines of Lewy Body Dementia* (Lindisfarne Books, 2016), 93. A previous version of this section appeared as "Alexander Dreier: In the Wild," *Arrowsmith,*

https://www.arrowsmithpress.com/journal/alexander-
dreier.

22. Dreier, *The Brain Is a Boundary,* 103.

23. Ibid., xvii.

24. Ibid., 74.

25. Ibid., 88.

26. John Matthews, ed. and trans., *Taliesin* (Aquarian Press,
1991), 296–300.

27. Ronald Dworkin, *Life's Dominion: An Argument
about Abortion, Euthanasia, and Individual Freedom*
(HarperCollins, 1993), 230.

28. György Lukács, *Soul and Form,* trans. Anna Bostock (MIT
Press, 1974), 153. Emphasis original.

29. See Barbara Hess, *De Kooning* (Taschen, 2004); Jerry
Saltz, "Definitive," *New York Magazine,* September 16,
2011, https://nymag.com/arts/art/reviews/de-kooning-
saltz-2011-9/; Mark Stevens and Annalyn Swan, *de Kooning:
An American Master* (Knopf, 2004); and Judith Zilczer,
A Way of Living: The Art of Willem de Kooning (Phaidon,
2023).

30. Paolo Colombo, ed., *In Praise of Shadows,* exh. cat. (Irish
Museum of Modern Art/Charta Books, 2008), 19–20.

V – DOMAINS OF VISION

1. Dave Goulson, *The Silent Earth: Averting the Insect
Apocalypse* (Vintage, 2021), cited in Edmund Gordon,
"Bye-bye Firefly," *London Review of Books,* May 12, 2022,
https://www.lrb.co.uk/the-paper/v44/n09/edmund-
gordon/bye-bye-firefly.

2. David Blayne Brown, Amy Concannon, and Sam Smiles,
eds., *J.M.W. Turner: Painting Set Free,* exh. cat. (J. Paul
Getty Museum/Tate, 2014), 25.

3. Fanny Moyle, *The Extraordinary Life and Momentous
Times of J.M.W. Turner* (Penguin, 2016), 410–12.

4. Brown, Concannon, and Smiles, eds., *Painting Set Free,* 158.

5. Moyle, *The Extraordinary Life and Momentous Times of J.M.W. Turner,* 411–12.

6. John Ruskin, *Modern Painters,* vol. 1, §38, available on *Project Gutenberg,* https://www.gutenberg.org/cache/epub/29907/pg29907-images.html.

7. Brown, Concannon, and Smiles, eds., *Painting Set Free,* 25.

8. Ibid., 27.

9. Ibid., 188.

10. Moyle, *The Extraordinary Life and Momentous Times of J.M.W. Turner,* 412.

11. Anthony Carlisle, *An Essay on the Disorders of Old Age, and on the Means of Prolonging Human Life* (Longman, Hurst, Rees, Orme, and Brown, 1818), 14.

12. Brown, Concannon, and Smiles, eds., *Painting Set Free,* 14.

13. James Hamilton, *Turner* (Random House, 1997), 378.

14. Brown, Concannon, and Smiles, eds., *Painting Set Free,* 17.

15. Daisy Indigenous Art, http://www.youtube.com/watch?v=RzgWMwYuHdY. This video is no longer available.

16. Roger Benjamin, ed., *Icons of the Desert: Early Aboriginal Paintings from Papunya,* exh. cat. (Cornell University Press, 2009), 32.

17. AGSA publication staff, "Loongkoonan," *Looongkoonan-AGSA, Art Gallery of Southern Australia,* 2016, https://www.agsa.sa.gov.au/whats-on/exhibitions/2016-adelaide-biennial-australian-art-magic-object/loongkoonan/.

18. Erin Parke, "105-Year-Old Kimberley Artist Daisy Loongkoonan Gathers International Acclaim," *ABC News,* April 11, 2016, https://www.abc.net.au/news/2016-04-11/105-year-old-kimberley-artist-gathers-international/7316168.

19. Shanna Collins, "This Indigenous Woman Took Up Painting in Her 90s, and Now She's World-Renowned," *Vibe,* September 23, 2016, https://www.vibe.com/features/viva/105-years-old-australia-aboriginal-artist-454284/.

20. Benjamin, ed., *Icons of the Desert,* 35.

21. Henry F. Skerritt, *Yimabowarra: The Art of Loongkoonan,* exh. cat., 2016, https://www.aamg-us.org/wp/wp-content/uploads/2016/03/Yimardoowarra_Fact_Booklet-sm.pdf.

22. Giuseppe Ungaretti, *Vita, poetica, opere scelte* (Il Sole, 2007), 197.

23. Charles de Tolnay, *Michelangelo: Sculptor, Painter, Architect,* trans. Gaynor Woodhouse (Princeton University Press, 1975), 42.

24. Ibid., 65.

25. Ibid., 168.

26. Paolo Portoghese, *Rome of the Renaissance* (Phaidon, 1972), 224.

27. Tolnay, *Michelangelo,* 122.

28. Douglas Penick, *The Age of Waiting* (Arrowsmith Press, 2020), 16–17.

29. BhP I.3.43. Cited in E.H. Rick Jarow, *Tales for the Dying: The Death Narrative of the Bhāgavata Purāṇa* (SUNY Press, 2003), 47. A previous version of this section appeared as "Endings," *Berfrois,* December 15, 2022, https://www.berfrois.com/2022/12/the-end-of-the-beginning-by-douglas-penick/.

30. BhP III.29.45. Jarow, *Tales for the Dying,* 58.

31. Adapted from Ramesh Menon, trans., *Bhagavata Purana* (Rupa Publications, 2007), 1409–10, and Gunada Charan Sen, *Shrimad Bhagavatam* (Munshiram Manoharlal, 1986), 190–91.

AFTERWORD

1. Dogen, "Moons," in *Abruptly Dogen,* ed. and trans. Smith, 65. A previous version of this section appeared as "Stravinsky at the End" *Arrrowsmith,* 2024, https://www.arrow-smithpress.com/journal/stravinsky-at-the-end.

2. Igor Stravinsky and Robert Craft, *Retrospectives and Conclusions* (Knopf, 1969), 24.

3. Matsuo Bashō, *Narrow Road to the Interior and Other Writings,* trans. Sam Hamill (Shambhala, 1991), 1.

Bibliography

Ackerman, James S. *Palladio*. Penguin Books, 1966.

AGSA publication staff, "Loongkoonan." *Looongkoonan-AGSA, Art Gallery of Southern Australia,* 2016. https://www.agsa. sa.gov.au/whats-on/exhibitions/2016-adelaide-biennial-australian-art-magic-object/loongkoonan/.

"2020 Alzheimer's Disease Facts and Figures." *Alzheimer's & Dementia* 16, no. 3 (2020): 391–460. DOI: 10.1002/alz.12068.

Bashō, Matsuo. *Narrow Road to the Interior and Other Writings.* Translated by Sam Hamill. Shambhala, 1991.

Beardmore, Thomas Marcus. "The Voice of Jean Rhys_0001. wmv." *YouTube,* November 17, 2012. https://www.youtube. com/watch?v=UN_6xJJNphY.

Beauvoir, Simone de. *Old Age.* Translated by Patrick O'Brien. Penguin Books, 1977.

———. *The Second Sex.* Translated by Constance Borde and Sheila Malovaney-Chevallier. Vintage, 2010.

"Beethoven and Rossini." *Popular Beethoven.* https://www. popularbeethoven.com/beethoven-and-rossini/.

Beethoven, Ludwig van. *Letters, Journals, Conversations.* Edited and translated by Michael Hamburger. Thames & Hudson, 1951.

Beltramini, Guido. *The Private Palladio.* Translated by Irena Murray and Eric Ormsby. Lars Müller, 2008.

Benjamin, Roger, ed. *Icons of the Desert: Early Aboriginal Paintings from Papunya.* Exh. cat. Cornell University Press, 2009.

Benjamin, Walter. "Robert Walser," translated by Rodney Livingston. In *Selected Writings,* Vol. 2, Part 1: *1927–1930,* edited by Michael W. Jennings, Howard Eiland, and Gary Smith. Harvard University Press, 1999.

Berenson, Bernard. *Sunlight and Twilight, from Diaries 1947–58.* Harcourt Brace, 1963.

Bernhard, Thomas. *Old Masters.* Translated by Ewald Osers. Penguin Books, 2020.

Blanqui, Louis-Auguste. *Eternity by the Stars: An Astronomical Hypothesis.* Translated by Frank Chouraqui. Contramundum Press, 2013.

Bornstein, George. "W.B.Yeats's Poetry of Aging." *The Sewanee Review* 120, no. 1 (2012): 46–61.

Blayne Brown, David, Amy Concannon, and Sam Smiles, eds. *J.M.W. Turner: Painting Set Free.* Exh. cat. J. Paul Getty Museum/Tate, 2014.

Cao Zhi [Ts'ao Chih]. "The Ruins of Lo Yang." Translated by Arthur Waley. In *One Hundred and Seventy Chinese Poems.* Knopf, 1919.

Carlisle, Anthony. *An Essay on the Disorders of Old Age, and on the Means of Prolonging Human Life.* Longman, Hurst, Rees, Orme, and Brown, 1818.

Centers for Disease Control. "About Dementia." August 17, 2024. https://www.cdc.gov/alzheimers-dementia/about/.

Certeau, Michel de. *The Practice of Everyday Life.* Translated by Steven Rendall. University of California Press, 1988.

Cézanne, Paul. "Letters from Paul Cézanne to Emile Bernard." *Art History Project.* https://www.arthistoryproject.com/artists/paul-cezanne/letters-from-paul-cezanne-to-emile-bernard/.

Clancy, Joseph P. *Welsh Medieval Poems.* Four Courts Press, 2001.

Clark, Kenneth. "The Artist Grows Old." *Daedalus* 135, no. 1 (2006): 77–90.

Collins, Shanna. "This Indigenous Woman Took Up Painting in Her 90s, and Now She's World-Renowned." *Vibe,* September 23, 2016. https://www.vibe.com/features/viva/105-years-old-australia-aboriginal-artist-454284/.

Colombo, Paolo, ed. *In Praise of Shadows.* Exh. cat. Irish Museum of Modern Art/Charta Books, 2008.

Coluga Pictures. "Are You A Turner Or A Constable Man-David Hockney outtake 23/80." *YouTube,* June 13, 2020. https://www.youtube.com/watch?v=mMNpqLk9CjM.

Danchev, Alex, ed. and trans. *The Letters of Paul Cézanne.* Getty Museum, 2013.

Dombrowski, André. "Impressionism and the Industrialization of Time." *Yale University Press,* January 5, 2024. https://yalebooks.yale.edu/2024/01/05/impressionism-and-the-industrialization-of-time/.

Dorival, Bernard. *Paul Cézanne.* Translated by H.H.A. Thackthwaite. Continental Book Center, 1948.

Dreier, Alexander. *The Brain Is a Boundary: A Journey in Poems to the Borderlines of Lewy Body Dementia.* Lindisfarne Books, 2016.

Dworkin, Ronald. *Life's Dominion: An Argument about Abortion, Euthanasia, and Individual Freedom.* Harper Collins, 1993.

Empson, William. "To an Old Lady." In *The Complete Poems,* edited by John Haffenden. Allen Lane, 2000.

Freud, Sigmund. "A Disturbance of Memory on the Acropolis (1936)." In *The Standard Edition of the Complete Psychological Works of Sigmund Freud,* Vol. XXII: *New Introductory Lectures on Psycho-Analysis and Other Works (1932–1936),* translated by James Strachey with Anna Freud. Hogarth Press, 1964.

Gawande, Atul. *Being Mortal: Illness, Medicine and What Matters in the End.* Profile Books, 2014.

"Georges Clemenceau and Claude Monet." *Georges Clemenceau's House.* https://www.maison-de-clemenceau.fr/en/discover/the-many-facets-of-georges-clemenceau/georges-clemenceau-and-claude-monet.

Gordon, Edmund. "Bye-bye Firefly." *London Review of Books,* May 12, 2022. https://www.lrb.co.uk/the-paper/v44/n09/edmund-gordon/bye-bye-firefly.

Goulson, Dave. *The Silent Earth: Averting the Insect Apocalypse.* Vintage, 2022.

Gregory, André. *This Is Not My Memoir.* Farrar, Strauss and Giroux, 2020.

Hallisey, Charles. "The Secret of a Woman of Ninety: Rethinking the Very Long Life." In *Rethinking the Human,* edited by J. Michelle Molina and Donald K. Swearer. Center for the Study of World Religions, Harvard Divinity School, 2010.

Hamilton, James. *Turner.* Random House, 1997.

Hayden, Ruth. *Mrs Delany: Her Life and Her Flowers.* British Museum, 1980.

Herbert, Robert L. "The Decorative and the Natural in Monet's Cathedrals." In *Aspects of Monet: A Symposium on the Artist's Life and Times,* edited by John Rewald and Frances Weitzenhoffer. Abrams, 1984.

Herbert, Zbigniew. "Apollo and Marsyas." In *The Collected Poems,* translated by Alissa Valles. HarperCollins, 2002.

Hess, Barbara. *De Kooning.* Taschen, 2004.

Jameson, Fredric. "Postmodernism, or the Cultural Logic of Late Capitalism." *New Left Review* 146 (1984): 53–92.

Janáček, Leoš. *Leoš Janáček's Uncollected Essays on Music.* Edited and translated by Mirka Zemanová. Marion Boyars Publishers, 1989.

Jarow, E.H. Rick. *Tales for the Dying: The Death Narrative of the Bhāgavata Purāṇa.* SUNY Press, 2003.

Jourdan, Pierre-Albert. *The Straw Sandals: Selected Prose and Poetry.* Translated by John Taylor. Chelsea Editions, 2011.

Jünger, Ernst. *A German Officer in Occupied Paris: The War Journals, 1941–1945.* Translated by Thomas S. Hansen and Abby J. Hansen. Columbia University Press, 2019.

Kohn, Eduardo. *How Forests Think: Toward an Anthtropology Beyond the Human.* University of California Press, 2013.

Larkin, Philip. "The Old Fools." *All Poetry.* https://allpoetry.com/The-Old-Fools.

Lévi-Strauss, Claude. *Wild Thought.* Translated by Jeffrey Mehlman and John Leavitt. Chicago University Press, 2021.

Lockwood, Lewis. *Beethoven: The Music and the Life.* W.W. Norton & Co, 2003.

Lukacs, Georg. *Soul and Form.* Translated by Anna Bostock. MIT Press, 1974.

Macauley, Wayne. "Nobody Should Be Afraid of His Little Bit of Weirdness: A Sideways Look at Robert Walser." *Syndey Review of Books,* October 24, 2014. https://sydneyreviewofbooks.com/essays/nobody-should-be-afraid-of-his-little-bit-of-weirdness-a-sideways-look-at-robert-walser.

Mallarmé, Stéphane. *Un coup de dés.* Translated by Anthony Hartley. Penguin, 1965.

———. *The Book.* Translated by Sylvia Gorelick. Exact Change, 2018.

"Mary Granville Delany: She Invented the Art of Mixed Media Collage at Age 71." *Later Bloomer.* https://laterbloomer.com/mary-granville-delany/.

Matthews, John, ed. and trans. *Taliesin.* Aquarian Press, 1991.

Menon, Ramesh, trans. *Bhagavata Purana.* Rupa Publications, 2007.

Merleau-Ponty, Maurice. "Cézanne's Doubt." In *Sense and Nonsense,* translated by Hubert L. Dreyfus and Patricia Allen Dreyfus. Northwestern University Press, 1964.

———. "Eye and Mind." In *The Merleau-Ponty Aesthetics Reader: Philosophy and Painting,* edited by Galen A. Johnson. Northwestern Univesoty Press, 1993.

——— *The Visible and the Invisible.* Translated by Alphonso Lingis. Northwestern University Press, 1968.

Milarepa. *The Hundred Thousand Songs of Milarepa.* Translated by Garma C.C. Chang. University Books, 1962.

Moyle, Fanny. *The Extraordinary Life and Momentous Times of J.M.W. Turner.* Penguin, 2016.

Panofsky, Erwin. *Meaning in the Visual Arts.* Anchor Books, 1955.

Parke, Erin. "105-Year-Old Kimberley Artist Daisy Loongkoonan Gathers International Acclaim." *ABC News,* April 11, 2016. https://www.abc.net.au/news/2016-04-11/105-year-old-kimberley-artist-gathers-international/7316168.

Peacock, Molly. *The Paper Garden.* Bloomsbury, 2012.

Penick, Douglas. "Gateways in Clouds: Stepping into Confusion." *Tricycle* (Spring 2022). https://tricycle.org/magazine/dementia-buddhism/.

———. *The Age of Waiting.* Arrowsmith Press, 2020.

Pizzichinni, Liliane. *The Blue Hour.* Norton & Co., 2009.

Portoghese, Paolo. *Rome of the Renaissance.* Phaidon, 1972.

Proust, Marcel, *In Search of Lost Time,* Vol. 6: *Time Regained.* Translated by Andreas Mayor and Terence Kilmartin. Revised by D.J. Enright. Modern Library, 2002.

Puett, Michael. "The Haunted World of Humanity: Ritual Theory from Early China." In *Rethinking the Human,* edited by J. Michelle Molina and Donald K. Swearer. Center for the Study of World Religions, Harvard Divinity School, 2010.

Rhys, Jean. *Wide Sargasso Sea.* Norton & Co., 1966.

Rosand, David. "Titian and the Critical Tradition." In *Titian: His World and His Legacy,* edited by David Rosand. Columbia University Press, 1982.

Ruskin, John. *Modern Painters,* Vol. 1. Available on *Project Gutenberg,* https://www.gutenberg.org/cache/epub/29907/pg29907-images.html.

Saltz, Jerry. "Definitive." *New York Magazine,* September 16, 2011. https://nymag.com/arts/art/reviews/de-kooning-saltz-2011-9/.

Scarry, Elaine. *The Body in Pain.* Oxford University Press, 1985.

Scranton, Roy. *Learning to Die in the Anthropocene: Reflections on the End of Civilization.* City Lights Books, 2015.

Sen, Gunada Charan. *Shrimad Bhagavatam.* Munshiram Manoharlal, 1986.

Silbergeld, Jerome. "Chinese Concepts of Old Age and Their Role in Chinese Painting, Painting Theory, and Criticism." *Art Journal* 36, no. 2 (1987): 103–14.

Skerritt, Henry F. *Yimabowarra: The Art of Loongkoonan.* Exh. cat. 2016. https://www.aamg-us.org/wp/wp-content/uploads/2016/03/Yimardoowarra_Fact_Booklet-sm.pdf.

Small, Helen. *The Long Life.* Oxford University Press, 2007.

Smith, Kidder, ed. and trans. *Abruptly Dogen.* punctum books, 2020.

Smith, Kidder, with Mike Zhai, trans. *Li Bo Unkempt.* punctum books, 2022.

Steer, John. *Venetian Painting: A Concise History.* Thames and Hudson, 1970.

Stevens, Mark, and Annalyn Swan. *de Kooning: An American Master.* Knopf, 2004.

Stevens, Wallace. "The Well Dressed Man with a Beard." In *Collected Poems of Wallace Stevens.* Alfred A. Knopf, 1971.

Stravinsky, Igor, and Robert Craft. *Retrospectives and Conclusions.* Knopf, 1969.

Tagore, Rabindranath. *Gitanjali.* Available on *Project Gutenberg,* https://www.gutenberg.org/cache/epub/7164/pg7164-images.html.

———. *Rabindranath Tagore on Art and Aesthetics.* Orient Longmans, 1961.

———. *The Meaning of Art.* Lalit Kala Akademi, 1983.

Thoreau, Henry David. *Walden.* Viking Penguin Books, 1983.

Tolnay, Charles de. *Michelangelo: Sculptor, Painter, Architect.* Translated by Gaynor Woodhouse. Princeton University Press, 1975.

Ungaretti, Giuseppe. *Vita, poetica, opere scelte.* Il Sole, 2007.

Vasari, Giorgio. *Lives of the Painters, Sculptors and Architects,* Vol. 4. Translated by A.B. Hinds. Dent, 1963.

Vu, Huong. "The Reflection of Age and Beauty in Titian's Late Style," edited by Miray Eroglu. *Canvas.* https://www.canvasjournal.ca/read/the-reflection-of-age-and-beauty-in-titians-late-style.

Waddington Hall Llanover, Augusta, ed. *The Autobiography and Correspondence of Mary Granville, Mrs. Delany,* Vol. 1, Second Series. Richard Bentley, 1862.

Walser, Robert. *Looking at Pictures.* Translated by Susan Bernofksy, Lydia Davis, and Christopher Middleton. New Directions, 2015.

————. *Microscripts.* Translated by Susan Bernofsky. New Directions, 2010.

Werth, Margaret. "Mallarmé and Impressionism in 1876." *Nonsite* 27 (2019). https://nonsite.org/mallarme-and-impressionism-in-1876/.

Wilhelm, Richard, and Cary F. Baynes, trans. *The I Ching or Book of Changes.* Princeton University Press, 1950.

Witkower, Rudolph. *Architectural Principles in the Age of Humanism.* Norton, 1971.

Wolf, Norbert. *I, Titian.* Translated by Ishbel Flett. Prestel Verlag, 2006.

Zemanová, Mirka. *Janáček: A Composer's Life.* Northeastern University Press, 2002.

Zemka, Sue. "Descent, Spirit, Heart, Senses." In *Literature and the Senses,* edited by Annette Kern-Stähler and Elizabeth Robertson. Oxford University Press, 2023. DOI: 10.1093/oso/9780192843777.003.0004.

Zilczer, Judith. *A Way of Living: The Art of Willem de Kooning.* Phaidon, 2023.